Are You Living Your Dream?

HOW TO CREATE WEALTH AND LIVE THE LIFE YOU WANT

John Fuhrman

Are You Living Your Dream?

JOHN FUHRMAN

Copyright © 2001 by John Fuhrman
FRAME of MIND, Inc. (888)883-3303
www.expertspeak.com
rejectme@aol.com
ISBN 0-938716-38-7

Published by
Possibility Press
e-mail: posspress@excite.com

Manufactured in the United States of America

Dedication

First of all, this book is dedicated to my wife, Helen, my son, John, and my daughter, Katie, and their dreams.

It is also dedicated to the new pioneers: those who are discovering the new frontiers of financial freedom. These people are the future of the world. They are the examples to follow. Their spirit is the incarnation of our forefathers and they are willing to share that spirit with all of us. When we have the dream and the fire to do what it takes, we can follow the trail blazed by these brave new explorers.

Other Books by *Possibility Press*

No Excuse!...Key Principles for Balancing Life and Achieving Success
No Excuse! I'm Doing It...How to Do Whatever It Takes to Make It Happen
No Excuse! The Workbook...Your Companion to the Book to
Help You Live the "No Excuse!" Lifestyle
Reject Me—I Love It!...21 Secrets for Turning Rejection Into Direction
If They Say No, Just Say NEXT!...24 Secrets for Going Through
the Noes to Get to the Yeses
The Electronic Dream...Essential Ingredients for Growing a
People Business in an e-Commerce World
Time And Money.com...Create Wealth by Profiting from
the Explosive Growth of e-Commerce
If It Is To Be, It's Up To Me...How to Develop the Attitude
of a Winner *and* Become a Leader
Get A GRIP On Your Dream...12 Ways to Squeeze More Success Out of Your Goals
Are You Fired Up?...How to Ignite Your Enthusiasm and
Make Your Dreams Come True
Dream Achievers...50 Powerful Stories of People Just Like You
Who Became Leaders in Network Marketing
Full Speed Ahead...Be Driven by Your Dream to Maximize
Your Success and Live the Life You Want
Focus On Your Dream...How to Turn Your Dreams and Goals Into Reality
SOAR To The Top...Rise Above the Crowd and Fly Away to Your Dream
In Business And In Love...How Couples Can Successfully
Run a Marriage-Based Business
Schmooze 'Em Or Lose 'Em...How to Build High-Touch
Relationships in a High-Tech World
SCORE Your Way To Success...How to Get Your Life on Target
What Choice Do I Have?...31 Choice Secrets to Help You Achieve
the Results You Want in All Areas of Life and Work
Dump The Debt And Get Free...A Realistic and Sensible Plan to
Eliminate Debt and Build Wealth in the 21st Century
Congratulations! You're A Millionaire!...The Secrets to Selling Your Way to a Fortune
Brighten Your Day With Self-Esteem...How to Empower, Energize and Motivate
Yourself to a Richer, Fuller, More Rewarding Life
Naked People Won't Help You...Keep Your Cool, Capture the
Confidence, and Conquer the Fear of Public Speaking

Tapes by *Possibility Press*

Turning Rejection Into Direction...A Roundtable Discussion With
Network Marketing Independent Business Owners

Contents

Acknowledgments

Thank you, Dr. Taylor Yates. You taught me patience. You must be an expert at it since you were dealing with me! And to your wife, Marsha, who just loved Helen and me from the day we met. Your teachings and example helped us to continue growing as people while our business grew.

Thank you, Tom and Cecile Brannon, Jen Dewing, and all the others we have come to know—you taught us enthusiasm and determination. Most of all, you taught us the importance of arriving, and that the time it takes to get there is irrelevant. Your willingness to drop everything and assist us is a shining example of how, with help, anybody can grow and succeed regardless of any obstacle.

Thanks to my family and everyone else who was patient with and supportive of me while I wrote and rewrote this book.

Thanks to the staff at Possibility Press for their tremendous sensitivity, creativity, and persistence in working with me to make this book all it has become.

I thank God for inspiring me with ideas and helping me change my focus from seeking personal gain to helping others, which is the key to all success.

Thanks to all of you for giving me more knowledge than I could have ever hoped for. With this book I can at least repay you in part for all you've given me.

And finally, I acknowledge you, the reader, for wanting to live your dream. I hope this book inspires you to do whatever it takes to make it come true. You can do it!

Why Would You Need This Book?

"Man does not simply exist, but always decides what his existence will be, what he will become in the next moment."
Viktor Frankl

Are you looking for more out of life? Or would you just like to get out of debt? Do you believe you're different than your fellow workers, who are satisfied with the status quo? Would you like a change in your life? Is looking for more just wishful thinking for those who aren't satisfied? Or has it become a necessity—something you're serious about?

Consider this: A recent poll showed that more people under age 35 believe in the likelihood of UFOs (Unidentified Flying Objects) than in the possibility of Social Security being around for them! In the next few years, the number of people over 65 years old who are still working will exceed the number of those who aren't working. The people who do manage to retire will have an average of less than $2,500 in the bank!

Most college grads today will have had a minimum of ten different jobs and three or four complete career changes before they can retire! That makes it virtually impossible to get vested and build a pension.

If you had the chance to significantly increase your income without affecting what you're doing, would that be of interest to you? If you had the chance to really build some wealth so you could live your dream, would you do something about it?

This book will give you some ideas to help you gain more control over your finances as well as other parts of your life. We'll look at some areas that you may be concerned about, and offer ideas for you to consider.

When you've finished reading this book, take some time to explore the possibilities for you and your family. Ask yourself, "What if I could make my dreams come true or just have a better life?"

Like anything worthwhile, this is not something for nothing. The more effort you put in, the greater your rewards can be. Of course you'll receive guidance, but no one will be watching over you like a boss, telling you what must be done. You and you alone decide where to take this. The purpose of this book is only to make you aware of the possibilities.

If you're looking for a get rich quick scheme, return this book to the person who lent it to you. Sure some people will achieve success more quickly than others, like in any field of endeavor, but that just doesn't matter. It's entirely up to you what you choose to do with it. Just do what's best for you and your family.

Over the last few decades, thousands of people have improved their financial picture and are living their dreams, thanks to what this book is about. I have included a few brief stories about some of them from a variety of backgrounds. Each story is unique and they all arrived at their own pace. Neither where they came from, nor how long it took them, really matters. It worked for all of them and it can work for you too. I am privileged to know some of them personally, and I'm also humbled by the example they set, where they came from, and what they have accomplished.

I believe this message will make a difference for you since you're now ready to make some changes in your life. My mission is to share it with as many people as possible so they, too, can live their dreams. It's important for you to realize that you also can live the life you want—it's not just for the privileged few. After all, if you don't have something to live and strive for, what's the point?

To be truly successful and happy in life, you need three basic ingredients—the desire or dream, a way to get it, and control over what you do. The fact that you're reading this book proves you have the desire and want more control. It'll give you the basics of a vehicle you can drive all the way to your dream.

As Sam Walton, founder of Wal-Mart once said, *"If you believe in your dreams, there's no limit to what you can do."* Locked up inside of you is a little kid who once thought anything was possible. As you grew older, however, you may have gotten mentally beaten up, if you will, and you and your ideas may have been put down.

Your dream of living the life you wanted may have, at some point, slipped away from you. And perhaps, here you are, not really as happy as you could be. Or worse yet, you may not be happy at all. However, there's still hope! The little dreamer you once were is still living inside you. All you need is the key to unlock the dreams in your heart. As Robert Browning once said, *"Our aspirations are our possibilities."* And believe it or not, our challenging situations are actually our opportunities in disguise!

In this book you'll find ideas, encouragement, and some information that can help you live your dream—before it's too late. You don't have forever you know. None of us do. Time waits for no one! If you've never been given a chance before, your luck has finally changed. This could be the chance you've been hoping for. Are you ready?

Successful people often say that *luck occurs when opportunity and preparedness meet.* The fact that you're reading this book says you are at least looking for an opportunity. Have you ever heard the Boy Scout motto, "Be prepared"?

Are you prepared for what could be the opportunity you've been waiting for? Are you ready to be lucky?

Imagine what your life could be like when you can do whatever you want to do, go wherever you want to go, buy whatever you want to buy, and be whatever you really want to be. Nobody is any better than you are. Sure some folks have different skills than you, but that doesn't mean they're more worthy than you. You have just as much right as anybody else to live the life you want!

Are you ready to make some changes in your life? Read these pages with an open mind and consider the possibilities for you and your family. Mark Twain may have said it best, *"Don't give up your dreams. When they are gone you may still exist, but you've ceased to really live."* Have you ever thought about that?

When we consistently go after our dreams, as the great philosopher Goethe once said, *"...all sorts of things occur to help one that would never otherwise have occurred...."* Many of the things you've always wanted that may have seemed to elude you are still within your reach. All you may need to do is develop greater expectations and beliefs, and associate with others who are moving on. Their support will make it easier for you to put more energy into achieving your dreams. Just believe that you can go as far as you can see yourself going, and maybe even beyond. That's what successful people do.

When you want and know you deserve a higher level of living, and start striving for your dreams, your whole world can change very quickly, if you want it to. It's all up to you. This book can show you the way, but only if you allow it to. The choice is yours.

If you're totally happy and satisfied with your life as it is, congratulations. You're one of the fortunate few. You've made a lot of good decisions and did a lot of the right things. If that's you, perhaps you know of someone who hasn't done so well, who would relish the chance to improve their lot in life. If so, you may want to share this book with them. It could be just what they've been looking for. You'll feel great having been able to share something with them that could really help them. They'll probably thank you for thinking of them.

So, get into your favorite easy chair, sit back, and relax. Give yourself some time to *really think* about how your life could be. If the person who shared this book with you gave you some other materials to review and maybe a couple of audio tapes to listen to, you may want to do that as well. You can then ask them any questions you may have. In fact, check them out thoroughly before you make any decisions. Sort it all out so you can determine what's best for you.

"Go after a dream with a sense of entitlement.
Know that you have the power to achieve it,
and that you deserve it...."
Les Brown

Introduction

*"Always bear in mind that your own
resolution to succeed is more important
than any other one thing."*
Abraham Lincoln

A s we venture into the world to make our mark, we need a toolbox. But true successes don't get that way by just showing off all their tools. They build success by *using them* to finely craft their mark. They then master certain tools and begin teaching others to do the same. Think of this book as a tool to help you craft your mark.

You can learn a great deal from this book. But your real education begins when the person who shared it with you shows you how to use it and the other tools in your box. Pay attention to this person. They can introduce you to some folks who can show you the ropes of success!

When I was discharged from the United States Navy, in 1976, several of my superiors were after me to re-enlist. To entice me, they tried to convince me I couldn't make it in civilian life. At the ripe old age of 21, I thought I knew all I needed to know to become successful. After all, I was a veteran. I felt that my country owed me a living and I was going to pick one that would make me rich! The first place I went to was the State Employment Office. (It could also be called the State Unemployment Office since everyone who uses it is out of work.)

They informed me that I didn't have to work, because as a veteran, I was entitled to six months of benefits. I didn't even have to go and pick the checks up—they'd mail them to me! I thought it would be great to sit at home and just wait for the money to flow right into my mailbox. After all, it was the exact amount I had earned in the Navy, and I got along fine on that. The only things I had to pay for were my food, clothes, and a place to live. But things were about to change—I was getting married!

I learned in the military that when you work harder you're rewarded with either time or money. Consistent hard work over long periods of time resulted in promotions in rank and a pay raise. And the longer you served, the more you received. Short-term rewards were also typical. If you worked a few extra hours over three or four days you were often rewarded with a 72- or 96-hour pass. Wow—you got a little bit of freedom!

In the working world of civilian life it seemed like they played by a different set of rules. I worked at a number of places, but I kept finding common themes at each that I didn't like. I offered to work more hours for more pay but was actually ignored because that would make the old timers look bad. Yet when I needed time off, I was often refused, even though I offered to work longer on other days.

I also found that even though I may have enjoyed the work, neither the environment nor some of my coworkers suited me. In some cases, I certainly wouldn't have chosen my particular boss had I had control over the situation. I soon figured out that if you wanted to survive, you needed to put up with a lot of stuff and fit in. You had to get by, by getting along. Sure, I wanted to make money, but I also wanted it to be enjoyable.

After a couple of years of putting up with all that nonsense, I started getting the itch to be independent. I talked it over with my wife and we decided that when I found something that didn't take much cash, I would do it.

One of my passions was scuba diving. Since I was an advanced diver and loved the adventure, I decided to open my own diving school and store. I also got something I hadn't had much of before—credit. I was extended enough credit to purchase the equipment to get started. I had it all—debt, overhead, and all the other strings that tie you to a conventional business.

I needed help, so I sought partners. They were as naïve as I was, but less honest. I went to instructor school to learn how to give lessons. While I was gone, equipment somehow began leaving my store but the payment for it never arrived! To make matters worse, I hadn't been putting any money aside to repay the loan for the equipment.

Then came the one thing that always happened where I lived. I never planned for it so no reserve was set up. It's called winter. No one in New Jersey wants to scuba dive in a January blizzard! I ended up going into bankruptcy. I also learned what, in my case, silent partners were and why they didn't want their name on anything. It was a hefty tuition to pay for a short course in business!

My wife and I then moved to New England to put that all behind us and start over again.

By 1984 I had been selling cars and making money. We were also expecting our first child. I kept working hard, getting raises, and getting promoted. When our son was just two years old, I made another decision. I was missing his growing up because of the 12-hour days and six-day work weeks. I needed more time with my family.

I decided to go into construction. I inquired about a home building business where the homes were built in prefabricated pieces and shipped to the site. All you needed to do was get the home put up and hand the keys over to the new owners. Before you could get involved, however, you were required to fly to South Carolina, tour the plant, and meet the people. If they liked you and you had the money, you could get an exclusive territory.

You needed to put one-third of the price of materials down and pay the balance within six months. No problem.

The economy and I were doing so well that I was in what seemed like the credit-card-of-the-week club. I carried $30,000 of credit in my wallet at all times. I went to the bank and took cash advances for the $8,000 down payment. Then I charged the tickets for my flight down. I also reserved a booth at the next home show.

The company was very good about leading you to believe you had the final say as to how you wanted to run your business. They even told me I could do business in most of New England. If anyone wanted one of these homes, they had to come to me. I was excited. I told my wife, this was a sure thing and that soon she would be a full-time mom and I would be home more often. It seemed like a dream come true.

As it turned out, in 12 short months, I had gone from earning almost $50,000 a year to a gross income of just over $4,000! Our credit card debt soared to almost $28,000, and we were using what limits we had left to pay the most overdue of the other credit cards. We hadn't made a mortgage payment in under 60 days late in almost nine months. To put the icing on the cake, they built one of my homes right around the block from where we lived. So much for it being my territory.

My wife wanted to talk to me and I was more nervous than I had ever been before. I finally understood how a mother reacts when anything threatens her children. She told me how much she loved me and wanted to continue to be supportive. She pointed out that I had tried to be on my own twice and failed. She was concerned, to say the least, that the children would suffer if I failed again. She wanted to protect our children. She was *not* happy with the situation I had put us in.

So, I went back to selling cars. After a few years, I was able to get a job as a professional sales trainer. This gave me a little more time and a lot more income. Even though I was in the top 2 percent of income earners in the country, it dawned on me that I could also be fired at anytime. Talk about being vulnerable.

Then a friend shared what this book is about, and something told me it was the right thing for me to do. I could grow a substantial secondary income with no capital risk, without leaving my job.

Well, before I had earned my fortune, the bubble burst on my dream job. Due to a huge personality conflict with a superior, I was no longer in the top 2 percent income bracket and they took away my company car. But because I took advantage of what you're soon to learn about, I was able to do three things: I got a brand new car for my wife, took the next three months off, and added on a new room for my son. We were also able to furnish my daughter's room, and I had time to write my first book. Most importantly, my wife is happy with me and glad I took a good look at this opportunity and did something with it.

What I am about to share with you may be just what you're looking for. Whatever you do, read this book and ask the questions you need to ask. Most importantly, look in the mirror and ask yourself, "Why should I do this?"

All you need is a dream for your future, the desire to have a better life, or to just pay off your credit cards and get out of debt. As you read, you'll discover how you can accomplish these things for yourself and your family. As an example, here's a brief story about a man who did.

Dexter and Birdie Yager—*Former Brewery Sales Rep and Data Entry Clerk*

"I was earning $95 a week before taxes when we came into the business...," he remembers. Dexter had been a car salesman and brewery representative. Birdie was a keypunch operator at an Air Force Base.

"It seems rather easy to understand that when two people are working toward the same goal, you get there faster, and certainly the effort required for two is less than required for one.... But if you're married to a winner and want that partnership to last, you have three choices: Get in gear and move to the top with him, get left behind, or hold both of you back...."

Dex and Birdie came from humble beginnings, but they had a dream for a better life. That coupled with the desire to help others who were willing to work toward their dreams, has rewarded them with an incredible lifestyle. Yet, family is also a priority with the Yagers. They are happy to report that three of their seven children are involved in various aspects of their business and their relationships are the best.

They live by and inspire others to realize, *"Success is the progressive realization of a worthwhile dream."* And Dex is known for saying, *"Don't let anybody steal your dream."*

No one lives forever. Isn't it high time for you to start living *your* dream? If not this, what? If not now, when? Read on and discover how you can make it happen for YOU.

Chapter 1
Time and Money

*"People often complain about
the lack of time when the lack of direction
is the real problem."*
John Fuhrman

Security or Freedom?

People can be divided into three groups. The successful group makes plenty of money but never seems to have any time to enjoy it. You know the type. They carry portable cell-phones and have beepers attached to their belts. Then there's Joe Average. He has plenty of time but not enough money to do what he really wants to do. Finally, you have those folks who seem to work all the time, yet never seem to have any money.

Does this sound familiar? If you work until age 65, and based on today's economic conditions that's optimistically young—you will have worked about 45 years. If you averaged two weeks vacation a year, that would be like working 43 years with less than two years off! Couple that with the fact that 95 percent of people 65 and older are either dead broke or dead, and it hardly seems like a fair deal. Why are we doing this to ourselves?

This routine gives most people a sense of security. They choose to work for someone else who, in effect, sets their income and lifestyle, rather than going out on their own to create the life they *really* want. Now, rather than criticize these folks, let's consider why they do it.

Eighty-three percent of all businesses fail within the first three years. Even though many people realize that having your own business is the key to financial independence, they simply aren't willing to put their security at risk. And of course, no one wants to be a part of some get rich quick scheme.

Being in any business is a serious endeavor and preparation and knowledge are important. Financing is often a major consideration too, especially if you're starting a conventional business. But what if there was a proven, simple business that anyone could do? A business that didn't require a financial risk and where there was someone to guide you every step of the way? If there was such a business, doesn't it make sense that you'd have a much better chance of succeeding at it?

Duplication—*A Revolution in Business*

In the late 1950s and early '60s just such an enterprise evolved. Using a proven formula for success, these businesses came with an owner's manual, training sessions, and field representatives. All the new operator needed to do was invest a modest amount of money and simply follow instructions. Their success was virtually guaranteed.

The process was called duplication and the industry was franchising. It went from a laughing stock to the Stock Exchange almost overnight. It was a business where other people learned from their mistakes, while eliminating most of the pitfalls by the time you came along. All you needed to do was *follow the system* and rake in the profits. It is one of the few businesses where product is actually secondary, and here's why:

When you think about it, who sells the most hamburgers in the entire world? McDonald's, right? Now ask yourself, have you ever had a better burger? Maybe, but there's more to it than that. McDonald's operates under *a system that insures success.* So what is a *system* and why is it so important?

Close your eyes for a minute. Picture yourself at a McDonald's. As you walk up to the counter, where are the fries made? Where are the soda machines? Where do they stack the burgers?

Years ago, when I was in Europe for the first time, I looked for something familiar, and spotted the golden arches. I was amazed at what I saw when I went inside. Everything was *exactly* the way it was back home. Why? Because they used a successful *system* which will work anywhere.

You may assume that franchising is a secure way to increase your income and give you the freedom not found with a job. However, the franchises that provide the most earnings are also the most costly. A McDonald's franchise, for instance, requires a total investment of anywhere from $433,000 to over $715,000! Now, it's true that not many of them fail. But if you had that kind of money to invest in something, you're probably already fairly secure. Why bother?

The more affordable franchises may also prove to be almost failure proof, but what is their potential for gain? A recent look at the Subway sandwich franchise, for instance, shows an extremely high success rate and moderate start-up costs. However, the average income for owners, after three years, is only around $50,000.

On top of that, the owners often work 80 hours a week and have the added responsibilities of employees, benefits, real estate, equipment, and big debt. It sounds like they might have bought themselves a job, with even longer hours than they had before! Is that what you're looking for?

Is There a Better Way?
What if you could take the ingredients that make franchises successful, eliminate the high investment costs, and provide direction for everyone to follow? You would have created an

opportunity that virtually anyone could do. The two most important ingredients are *duplication* and the *system*.

Unlike franchises, *duplication* of the *system* you're learning about can be done by anyone—regardless of age, educational, economic, or social background. It allows everyone to grow at their own speed, based on what they want to accomplish and how much effort they choose to put in. This *system* helps people get on the right track the instant they start. By *duplicating* this *system* you can operate more effectively and efficiently than a franchise, while creating personal wealth and time freedom.

If there were only one McDonald's restaurant in the world, the operator would make a decent living. But by *duplicating* the process over and over again, with thousands of other McDonald's owners, billions of hamburgers have been sold. As a result, Mrs. Ray Kroc gets wealthier every day of her life regardless of whether she personally works or not! Their *system of duplication* is self-perpetuating.

By sharing the process of *duplication with others*, you too can take advantage of the potential. By having others duplicate your efforts, it's possible for you to enjoy the rewards of doing more than you could do alone. Even though you physically may put in only 2 to 3 hours a day, duplication can give you the effect of working 100 to 1000 hours (or more) a day! How would you feel being in a situation like that?

By *duplicating the system* I'll share with you soon, you can create both wealth and security. When others duplicate what you do, similar to what each McDonald's restaurant does, you're actually diversifying your sources of income. And this is where true security comes from—just ask anyone who's wealthy.

Chapter 2
Residual Income— The Great Secret of the Rich!

"The only way to become financially and time free is to have a permanent ongoing income that keeps coming in long after you did the work to establish it."
John Fuhrman

Do the Work Once and Keep Getting Paid!

Did you know that Elvis Presley's estate earns more money today than he earned while he was alive? Are you aware that a successful inventor develops their device once, then when it's manufactured and distributed, they continue to receive a royalty on each unit sold? Would you believe Frank Sinatra's estate is still receiving income from songs he recorded half a century ago?

These people put faith in the *process of duplication*. They didn't know what the exact reward would be, but they knew it could continue year after year, long after the work they did to earn it! That's called *residual income*. It's the great secret of the rich, and it can set you free!

What if there's something you could do part-time, for the next two to five years, where you could create a permanent walk-away income, without affecting what you're currently doing? Would you like to create a permanent residual income that is also self-perpetuating for the life of the business? Not only will it continue paying you but it can also grow—long after you've stopped doing it! And when you keep doing it, you can *add to* what you already have coming in. That's how many of the rich keep getting richer!

For example, Dave Thomas, founder of Wendy's, could retire tomorrow. If he did, do you think they would stop opening new Wendy's restaurants around the world? Of course not. The beauty of it is, he'll continue to get a percentage of their increasing profits! This type of income has other benefits as well.

What if You Couldn't Work or Worse?

Suppose, for a moment, you're a man with a wife, two children, a mortgage, and car payments. If something would happen to you where you were no longer able to work, where would the money, that used to be your income, come from? If you died, which one of your family members would inherit your job? Oh, you may say, "I have plenty of insurance to handle that." But let's see just what plenty means.

A study was done on the insurance coverage of the average married man. Here's what it showed:

Age – 37
Income – $32,500
Mortgage – $80,000
Auto loan – $11,000
Installment debt (credit cards, etc.) – $5,000
Dependents – 2 kids

What do you suppose this average man has for insurance coverage? Compare this with your own coverage. The answer is only $17,000. Could your family survive?

Just suppose for a moment he can afford higher premiums and has $200,000 worth of insurance. Surely that would be enough. I did the following fictitious scenario with my wife to see where the money would go. Here's what she did:

First, she's very considerate. She buried me; cost – $6,000. The next day, she paid off the mortgage; cost – $80,000. She knew that the most important thing lost (besides me!) was my income. Smartly, she put aside one year's worth; cost – $32,000.

To feel more secure, she also paid off the car and the installment debt; cost – $16,000. Like many parents, she wanted to make sure our children were able to attend college. Even a state college is expensive. So, she put aside $20,000 per child for school; cost – $40,000.

Now add it all up. She had only $26,000 left to bring up two children and get through the rest of her life. She spent a grand total of $174,000 within days of the funeral! Now, keep in mind, this is based on $200,000 worth of coverage! We haven't even begun to consider things like food, clothing, and care for the kids while she goes out to find a job to replace the lost income.

How do you stack up? What would happen to your family if you were taken out of the picture? What kind of financial situation have you set up for your family?

The Power of Residual Income

Let's say you don't have that much insurance coverage but you do have a residual income that is also inheritable. Would that make a difference in your family's life? What if you could create a cash flow that continues paying and growing regardless of your presence on this earth? How secure would you feel then? Is there enough life insurance to generate that type of cash flow? Yes, but you would have to cut back on your current lifestyle to afford the premium! And who wants to cut back? I sure don't. Do you?

That's the power of residual income. If you're like most people who've read this far, you, too, may be asking yourself, "How could I possibly set up a permanent, residual income for myself and my family?" Here are a few ways you could consider:

1) Invent a product people will purchase forever.
2) Record an all-time, bestselling album.
3) Start a franchise destined to become the next McDonald's.
4) Capitalize on coming trends and fill the needs of consumers.

Which one do you believe best fits your personality, talent, and resources? If you're gifted or wealthy enough to do one of the first three, congratulations. There's no sense for you to continue reading this book. Best wishes for your future. But perhaps you know someone who could benefit from this book and you'll pass it on to them.

However, *if what you have to offer is some time, ambition, and your own dream, what follows may be the answer you've been searching for.*

You're probably asking yourself, "How much residual income do I need to become financially independent?" To answer that, you need to understand what true financial freedom is. It's not just income that sets you free. You need to also consider your outgo. If you earn a million dollars a year but pay all but $5,000 to debt and obligations, you're at the same level of freedom as the person who earns $35,000 a year and pays out $30,000! You're just broke at a higher lifestyle.

As long as debt controls what you need to earn, you're not free. Once you find the right vehicle, it's how diligently you work at it that'll largely determine how quickly you can get out of debt and become financially free. Remember, success comes before work only in the dictionary.

Rapid Debt Reduction
Regardless of whether you're up to date on all your bills, residual income could be your ticket to freedom. Would you

like to start right now on your path to financial freedom? If so, then while you're still making the same amount of money as you have been, begin practicing *delayed gratification*. Wait to get the extras until you're in a financial position to enjoy them *free and clear*. Don't spend the next few years working to pay the stuff off, prospering the bank and credit card companies, rather than yourself. Those folks already have enough of your money! Enough is enough, already.

Let's say you're earning $30,000 a year and paying $1,000 a month to service your debt. How about putting your efforts into creating enough residual income to pay off all your debts within a year? What would the following year look like? Well, for one thing, you could put $12,000 in the bank. Or you could bank half and use the other half for a nice vacation. Would you like that kind of freedom?

Just suppose you recently obtained a mortgage on a new home. The monthly payment is $1,000 and you're making $1,000 a month residual income in addition to your regular pay. Add that extra $1,000 of residual to your mortgage payment and you'll be amazed at what happens.

Assuming you took a 30-year mortgage and you doubled the payments, how soon do you think it would be paid off? Most people guess 15 years. The truth is you'd own your home free and clear in only 6½ years!

Just suppose, after 6½ years, you continued making the mortgage payment amount *to yourself*, putting it in your own bank account (rather than the mortgage loan account), while living on the income from your regular job. Also imagine that you spent your residual income on fun things. You'd still end up with $282,000 in the bank after 30 years. If you also banked the residual payments, the total would be $564,000! With interest compounding over the same time, you'd have almost $1,000,000! And remember, your residual income still continues.

When you own your home free and clear, have nearly $1,000,000 in the bank, and have a steady extra income of $1,000 a month, how free are you? A lot freer, right? That's the power of residual income and how it can lead to rapid debt reduction!

What Creates Residual Income?

Let's use McDonald's again as an example. The question is "Where does the residual income come from?" Say you had the money and opened your own McDonald's franchise. If you followed their system, it's highly likely you would have a successful operation. Your success however, would be limited by your own time and effort, which will include supervising and managing employees in addition to working for yourself. Since there are only 24 hours in a day, you can only do so much. And that's what limits your success!

Now, just suppose you've helped a few others get their own franchises started. In this case your first franchise would be called a Master Franchise. Every franchise you help develop beyond that would be an offshoot of your original franchise. They would provide you with an ongoing percentage of *their* profits. As long as they operate, you make an income from all the money *they* bring in.

Your success and income begin to multiply because you expanded the overall operation by helping others succeed in theirs. You would literally multiply the results of your efforts while still physically not working any more than you were when you just had your own franchise!

The key to financial independence and time freedom is, first of all, finding the right income vehicle for you. When you help enough people get what they want, you'll be able to get what you want. Your income will be determined by how many people you help get their own business started and running successfully. The more people you help to do this, the larger your income will be. By helping them make more, you make more. It's a true win-win situation.

Now, just suppose you encourage the people you helped to go out and help others get started. Now, your residual income begins to compound even faster. In fact, you could get to the stage where you no longer needed to personally run your own franchise. All you would then be doing is helping those who are helping others get started. *This is what many super successful people do, regardless of what type of business they're in.*

J. Paul Getty, formerly the richest man in the world, once said, "I would rather have (the results of) 1 percent of the effort of 100 men than that of 100 percent of my own." Makes sense, doesn't it? With residual income from duplication, you're building security by not placing all your eggs in one basket. If a few of those people you've helped don't become as successful as you thought they would, you still have plenty of others to keep things going. If you had only one enterprise and it began to fail, you would be hard pressed to succeed.

When those people, whose efforts are generating residual income for you, also believe in the power of duplication, they're likely to begin the process over again for themselves. When you help them achieve a certain level of income, you'll receive a royalty based on their efforts and the profits they generated. Your helping them succeed does not detract from their income, but rather adds to their earnings, so the incentive to keep growing never goes away. Furthermore, the more you help them earn, the more you earn! It's a win-win relationship—the kind that benefits each of you.

Chapter 3
Sharing Is a Great Way to Succeed

"By giving, you receive."
John Fuhrman

Could You Use an *Additional* $3,000 a Month?

What if you had an opportunity to earn an extra $3,000 a month? This is in addition to your regular job or business earnings and it keeps coming in no matter what happens to your employment or business situation. How would you feel? Can you see that happening? How does that sound to you? Would that help you change some things in your life or, at least, increase your standard of living? *Imagine how it would be to put money into your checking account and be able to leave it there or transfer it to savings!* For anyone living from paycheck to paycheck, that, in and of itself, would probably be a dream come true.

How Would You Like to Create Some Financial Options?

For some folks $3,000 a month isn't a lot of money, while for others it may be equal to or greater than their current income. But consider this: *By following the success system this book covers, you can have significant income growth without giving up your current occupation.* As a result, it can also help you create new options for yourself.

If you are getting by or even living comfortably on your current income, what would an extra $3,000 a month mean to you? Would you live in the same home? Would your kids go to the same school? Would the pressure of trying to figure out how to afford retirement be eased a little? Would celebrating birthdays and holidays be easier and more enjoyable? Would it help with college tuition? Would it enable you to contribute to your favorite charity? When you have more financial options you can more easily pursue one or more of these ideas or others. And you can actually have fun with them!

Do You Know Three "Hungry" People?

Now what if I said this was only the tip of the iceberg? The real big money, the residual income, comes from duplication. By introducing people to this system, you could put yourself in a situation where you would never have to work for someone else ever again. Sound too simple? It is simple and, like anything worthwhile in life, it requires effort.

Most people could retire on the residual income generated from three enterprises, each earning $3,000 a month. That's the simple part. Find three people who need and want to earn that kind of additional income, and are willing to work for it, and you can be on your way.

Who Wants to Earn Extra Money?

You feel good about your future. You can picture yourself being a full-time parent or doing something else you enjoy due to your newfound financial freedom. Your prospects of making your dreams come true are getting better and better every day. However, you still need to find three people who are serious about wanting more out of life, or who would even just like to get out of debt. There are 275 million people in the United States alone. Surely there must be three who want to improve their financial picture and will do what it takes to make it happen! Take your pick.

Picture yourself in a park where there are hundreds of pigeons. By the looks of them you can tell they haven't eaten in days and they're on the brink of starvation. You brought along a bag of birdseed and you're all ready to feed them. Now, take a handful out of your bag and begin running toward them. Scream that you have their salvation and they need to eat it. What do you suppose will happen? Do you think these starving birds will stay around and eat? Nope! They'll use their last ounce of strength to fly away from you and maybe even die as a result. The trouble is, that approach doesn't work. You ended up scaring them off from the thing they wanted the most!

Does that make any sense? Here you are with the answer to a life-threatening problem and they just fly away. So, what's the solution to this apparent dilemma? It's all in the *approach*. When you gently walk over to a park bench, sit down, and throw out some seeds, chances are the birds will come and eat. Some of them may even eat right out of your hand! They are more likely to trust you because of your gentle approach.

People respond similarly. If you run toward them saying you have the answers to all their problems, they'll probably fly away too. They're likely to start coming up with reasons (excuses) why they don't need you or your ideas. They may say things like, "I'm doing okay," "Money isn't everything," or "I don't have time." There are more, but one excuse is as good as another. It's just human nature to shy away from something that seems too good to be true, especially if the person sharing it seems too eager!

So What's the Best Way to *Approach* People?

The approach you take when you're sharing an opportunity with someone is key. It could mean the difference between becoming successful or living an average "same old, same old" life. When you share the opportunity the way the system teaches, with people who are serious about achieving their goals and dreams, you can dramatically increase your chances of succeeding. By now, you're probably asking yourself, "How can I find three people interested in significantly increasing their income without affecting their current job or business?"

To begin with, most people *are* interested in increasing their income. But some people are naturally skeptical of opportunity, and rightly so. It's well-known that there are many scams and so-called get rich quick schemes out there. Some folks may have even lost money from one of these in the past. These people generally need to know two key things: First, they need proof it can be done. And second, they need to be shown how it's done. For example, no one would buy a McDonald's franchise without knowing these two things! They'd be foolish if they did.

Do you think McDonald's began franchising from day one? No way! Before they could do that, they made lots of mistakes which gave them the opportunity to iron out all the bugs. Once they developed a proven system for success, they began telling other people that they, too, could do it. They then showed them how it's done, and helped those that asked how to get started.

This opportunity is similar. Prove to people they can do it and let them learn how to do it. Show them how to get started or introduce them to someone who can. When people know help is available and, more importantly, others are interested in seeing them succeed, they're more likely to feel good about the opportunity, whatever it may be.

For example, say you have three people who have a sincere desire to earn $3,000 more a month. One of the ways to help these people get started is to show them some people who've already done it. When a new McDonald's is bought, there's no money coming in. In fact, the owner is probably in the hole financially, because of the huge investment required. However, the new owner believes they'll succeed because, before they invested any of their money, they've seen many other McDonald's who have succeeded. Their natural skepticism led them to check it out before they could feel good about their decision to go ahead.

Everyone who starts a duplication business faces the same challenge. How do you prove to others they can earn extra money, when you're just getting started yourself? It may sound like a "Catch 22" situation, but it's not. First, be sincere, then others are more likely to listen. It doesn't matter that you may never have been in business before. Whether you have or you haven't, simply introduce your potential associate to somebody who's successful in this business. Show them that the golden arches, so to speak, really do work. The person who shared this book with you can help you with that.

In Business for Yourself, but Not by Yourself

One of the great things about the duplication business is that there's plenty of help available. Those who are earning the kind of income you desire are more than happy to share with you how they did it. They're the proof this works, while your enthusiasm is what sparks the interest of those you want to work with. There are successful people who can help you share the idea with others who want more income and are willing to work for it. Even though you're relying on their expertise, *you* benefit because it was *you* who approached your potential business associates and generated their interest in learning more.

Now, why would someone want to help you? *A core principle of any success in life is that it hinges on your helping or leading others to success!* This is a true win-win situation. Truly successful people make it a priority to create circumstances where everyone involved benefits. Fortunately, you can learn from their experience. Use them as success models for yourself, as well as for those you choose to share your opportunity with.

Who Could I Share It With?

Here's an example of who may be interested: A friend of a business associate and I were having lunch. He had been in his industry for a long time and was beginning to resent the long hours he had to work to be successful in that field. And even though he had a great income, he didn't like being away from his family so much. His kids seemed to be growing up without him. He said to me, "If I could find a way to earn an extra $1,000 a month, I'd give up this crazy business and get a job with more humane hours." If you heard this and had an excellent opportunity to offer him, wouldn't you do it? He's sure ripe for one. Now he's building this business with me!

Think back to your youth. Did you and your friends ever plan careers that would keep you together? Who would you like to spend more time with?

Since you're older now, you've probably also made some new friends you'd like to spend more time with. You may even want to share this opportunity with them. Whether or not they choose to do anything with it themselves, true friends will always support you in your decision to move on.

Another great benefit of this business is that you'll have more choices. Most of us can't pick our boss or coworkers. As long as we choose to work there, we're probably stuck working for and with whomever the company assigns. But when you're in business for yourself you can *choose* with whom you'd like to associate. If there are people you'd feel uncomfortable working with, don't share your opportunity with them. *You get to select or reject who you'll talk to about it.* It's up to you. You're in the driver's seat.

Jerry and Peggy Boggus—*Former Army Captain and Homemaker*

In Jerry's case, the mountain-like hurdle was his own lack of self-confidence. "For so long I had put such importance on titles," Jerry shares, "but when I finally realized that everyone needs something which the opportunity afforded, I began to develop better self-esteem. I faced my own insecurities and was thrilled at being able to conquer my fear of dealing with people one on one."

Peggy explains further, "We were loners. We never did go out looking for friendship. Through this business we began changing, reaching out to others, and realizing some personal goals."

"I love sharing this business," relates Jerry emphatically. "I truly enjoy seeing that light in people's faces when they realize there IS hope after all. That makes everything worthwhile."

Chapter 4

Duplication—How to Be Productive With an Hour a Day

"Give me a lever long enough, and I can move the world."
Archimedes

One Percent of the Effort of 100

Let's see. You probably work, take care of the kids, keep up the house and yard, and, with whatever time's left, you sleep. Sounds like a full plate. How could you ever hope to put yourself in a situation that can produce the income you need to enjoy the life you're working so hard to have? Simple. You need two things to get started—one hour a day and one of the most powerful ways to build wealth on the planet.

Wait a minute. An hour a day? How can anyone develop much of a secondary income on an hour a day?

J. Paul Getty's statement is worth repeating, *"I would rather have (the results of) 1 percent of the effort of 100 men than 100 percent of my own."* Why do you suppose one of the wealthiest men in the world would have said that? He understood the power of this wealth builder—that the efforts of many are far more powerful than that of one.

Consider this: Suppose you had 1 percent of the results from each of 100 people and one of them became ill. You would still be operating at 99 percent! On the other hand, what if you chose to do it all by yourself and you got sick? What can you hope to accomplish with 0 percent?

What's this powerful "secret" that's created more wealth than all the gold and oil strikes in history combined? Once again, as in the case of McDonald's, it's called *duplication*. It's been used by the power brokers and the captains of industry since the beginnings of free enterprise. *Duplication* is simply a way of *leveraging* yourself and it's available to everyone. All you need to do is use it. And of course, it's up to you what you decide to do with it.

How Does *Duplication* Work?

The best way to learn is to share what you know with others. When you put this idea into practice, using this system, you can experience the magic of duplication and grow a powerful enterprise. Many other people have done it, and so can you.

Say you commit to following this system for a year. Also imagine you have no more than one hour a day to devote to it. Picture creating a situation where you could afford to retire from what you're doing, if you want to. Then imagine how you might do that with only an hour a day. Sounds impossible, doesn't it?

Here's the key: For an hour a day, search for people who have dreams and desires like you do and who are serious about making them come true. Be sure to ask the person who shared this book with you how to approach such people, if they haven't already showed you. When you find some people with those qualities who you'd like to share this opportunity with, follow the recommended approach. Once they're interested in learning more about the opportunity they'll have the chance to share it with others as well. Now, do you understand how you can generate significant additional income by investing an hour a day? If you're still not sure, don't worry. Most people feel the same way.

Suppose all you can do with your hour a day is find only one person who's interested in living a better life and who's willing to do something about it. To be conservative, let's say it took you an entire month to find this person. That's terrific. After all, even McDonald's probably didn't grow that fast when they first started.

Perhaps this person will be able to devote more than an hour a day to this business. But let's say that's not the case; all they have is an hour a day that they can use to follow this system. Much to your surprise, you now have a situation where two whole hours a day are being invested in your business—your hour plus the one your new friend and associate has! Congratulations. *You've just doubled what you can do!* You've just experienced the power of leverage through duplication, just like many people who become very successful.

Say your person is excited about this opportunity and they start sharing it with others. Let's say they're a good student of the business. Where do you suppose you would be if you could find one such person a month and each one did what you did? Can you picture your bank account growing bigger and bigger?

Here's what happens after the second month: In addition to your original person, you find another. Now you have two, right? Nope! The person you originally shared the opportunity with went ahead and shared it with someone else! Almost before you realized what was going on, you made it possible, either directly or indirectly, for three others to each get started in their own independent business. Furthermore, they are a part of your business as well, and that's something you can really get excited about!

Let's continue conservatively, assuming that no one ever has more than one hour a day to devote to their business. In another month you could have a total of eight people, each sharing the idea. As they do so, some of the people they share it with will choose to start their own business. Others, however, will prefer just to buy at a discount or be retail clients and take advantage of the convenience of shopping at home, saving time and money buying many of the products they now buy at stores.

At this point, you have leveraged yourself to where your business is operating eight hours a day, for your one. If your business would continue to expand at this rate, you'd have 4,096 households either investing time in their businesses or just consuming products at a discount or as retail clients.

Does It Really Work That Way?

The above example is great in theory but in reality it doesn't work that way. It's a well-known fact that something like 80 percent of all businesses fail within the first year. But let's be conservative and say 95 percent fail and only 5 percent keep going. That would still leave you with over 200 people in *your* business as they invest time in their own or just use products. You could be generating a substantial permanent income depending on how your business was structured and the volume of products moved and consumed each month.

If the average household uses anywhere between $100 and $500 worth of products a month, your business would be doing between $240,000 and $1,200,000 a year in volume. That's a nice little business. And, of course, the great thing is, you get paid a percentage of all this volume in a monthly check! If you receive, say, a 5 percent overall bonus on your total business volume, you'd be making somewhere from $12,000 to $60,000 a year in extra income.

Why do people fail? One big reason is that they just *try*. While you are striving for a change in lifestyle, you need to *do*, not just try. You also need to do exactly what you want others to duplicate. Fortunately, the system is in place to help you do just that.

What's Good for the Goose Is Not Always Good for the Gander!

Say you want a strong additional income and decide to make it happen. You've committed to getting it done as quickly as possible and you're willing to do whatever it takes. To maximize your growth potential, just do what other people can duplicate. That may be to simply call people on the phone. That's something others who are duplicating you can do—virtually everyone has a phone. Just do what the system recommends as easily duplicatable so more people can do it.

The flexibility of this opportunity allows you to share it with people right in your own home. Duplicatability is key here too. Imagine having a couple over who are bright, ambitious, "perfect" in every way, and excited about living their dream. They both work and have two young children to provide for. They arrive at your house, appreciative that you're offering them a chance for a better life.

When you open the door, you greet them with a smile. After everyone's comfortably seated, you might ask if they'd like coffee or something. After you've spent the evening with them, they look at each other and realize, they could easily do this. Had you prepared a fancy meal, using your best china and crystal, you might have scared them off. Duplicating that would have been expensive and time consuming.

The key to your success, before you do anything relating to the business, is to ask yourself, "Can anyone duplicate this part simply and inexpensively?" If the answer is no, don't do it. Everything you do in the business needs to be as easy to duplicate as possible. When you follow the system, your business has the best chance of growing quickly and securely.

One of the main qualities to look for in an associate is their teachability. People who've become successful in conventional businesses may think they know what to do in this business. Other than using good people skills, this is usually not the case.

People who may "know it all" in their business or occupation can only succeed in this business when they follow the system. They can be very successful simply by listening to those who have already succeeded!

The key is to share things that can be easily learned and duplicated. Nothing could be simpler than this fact and it's the cornerstone of your income and its growth. The simpler it is for people to duplicate what you do, the better your chances are that more people will relate to you and the opportunity you have to offer them. And, of course, the more people you share this with and build relationships with, the larger and more prosperous your business can become.

This business can help you live the life you want and deserve. How long it takes will largely depend on you and the effort you put into it. Many folks have reached their goals within two to five years. It's entirely up to you what you do with it. It's your choice.

Don and Nancy Wilson—*Teacher/Coach and Nurse*

After a successful basketball and baseball college career, Don became a popular high school science teacher and head basketball coach. Nancy was busy as a registered nurse, homemaker, and mother. Neither had time to build this business.

"It took us a while to get going," Nancy recalls, "but it wasn't long before we both realized that we desperately wanted to beat the mental and financial bondage that most people live under all their lives. We wanted something better, even if it meant learning how to use our time more efficiently."

That limited time in the beginning was put to good use. By leveraging their efforts through helping others succeed, Don and Nancy have built a huge business that takes them all over the world.

"Best of all," adds Nancy, "our children have parents who are free. That means more than all the material things. If we achieved only that, the freedom would make everything worthwhile!"

Chapter 5
Diversify Yourself to Freedom

"Don't put all your eggs in one basket."
Author Unknown

The Great Protector

What's the safest way to invest in the stock market? Many people choose mutual funds. Some of you may ask, "What are they?" They're a collection of stocks from different companies. For example, a utility fund invests in the stocks of utility companies around the country. You could do this yourself, but you wouldn't have the buying power they have. One of the main reasons many are so successful is because they don't rely on just one stock.

They protect their investors by being diversified. If one stock sharply decreases in value, the blow isn't severe enough to hurt the fund. You don't have to know everything about every company in the portfolio to feel safe. These experts hedge their bets by purchasing a mix of stocks in tune with what their investors hope to accomplish. They diversify.

Corporations also use diversification as protection. Many who are at their peak purchase companies that aren't related to their industry. This enables them to weather a storm. If the stock of one company goes down, it may be rising in another. Corporations are sometimes able to purchase other companies when their stocks are down so that when they rise, the purchasing company experiences huge profits.

Diversification, simply put, is not putting all your eggs in one basket. Many of us already do that in many areas of our lives. We may have more than one bank account, more than one credit card, several different stores we shop at, more than one car, and so on. Since most people aren't independently wealthy, how come more of us don't diversify what is one of the most important facets of our lives—our source of income?

Most of us were taught to go to school, get good grades, get a good job, and work there for the rest of our lives. Sure sounds like all our eggs are bumping around in one basket, doesn't it?

Why is it so easy to accept diversification in other areas of our lives, yet when it comes to our income we may have chosen to limit ourselves to only one source? This makes even less sense when you realize that if you work for someone else your employer has probably diversified the workload by hiring various people. If it's good enough for them, isn't it good enough for you too?

Why Did I Diversify?

After a brief stint in the military, I began my civilian career selling cars. After a while, I became very successful at it. As a matter of fact, I was in the industry for over 15 years. However, a few years back, we were hit with a huge recession. As good as I was, it became very difficult to sell vehicles to those who were out of work or about to be laid off.

Regardless of my talent, things beyond my control prevented me from earning a decent living. If I had had another source of income, I might have been able to stick it out until the business got better.

At that time, a company servicing car dealers was looking for someone to service their accounts and develop new ones. It offered a base salary, an expense account, and commissions. Sounds secure, doesn't it? I took the job and grew the territory to one of the most successful in the country.

At the same time, someone offered me the very opportunity you're reading about. Since I was getting a big league salary, I figured I didn't need the money. I did learn about and understand diversification though. And I really liked the sincerity of the person showing me this opportunity. So, I got started.

Regardless of my previous experience with success in the car business, the one thing I didn't anticipate was a negative reaction from a key player. As my success became more recognized by both the company and my dealers, jealousy began to surface. The surprise was that the one who became jealous was the same person my success benefited the most—my boss! Before I knew it, I was history from a job where I was a top producer.

This job was a specialty. There weren't more than a handful like it in the whole country. Even if another such job was available, I didn't want to relocate my family. Under normal circumstances, this could have put my lifestyle in jeopardy.

However, when I began that job four years earlier, I had also started a duplication business which enabled me to diversify and create residual income. I learned the principles of financial management that allowed me to leave a great job with absolutely no financial pressure, take four months off, and write my first book.

How would you feel if your boss came in tomorrow and said you were no longer employed? Could you drive home from your old job, hug your spouse (if you have one), and go pick out a new car? I did. And so can you!

Does Your Current Income Provide the Security for Your Family That You'd Like?

When I was still selling cars, my son was only six years old and my daughter was a newborn. What if something had happened to me on the way to work? How would they have managed? Yes, I had life insurance. However, my son was still going to be financially dependent on the family income for another 12 to 15 years and my daughter for 18 to 22 years. How far do you think life insurance would take you under those circumstances? Maybe they could inherit my job? How many infants and children have you seen selling cars?

By diversifying my sources of income, the residual income my business generates will be paid to my heirs for years to come. Plus, as the kids get older they can build an even bigger business of their own, which is also part of my business, to leave to their kids. This could also substantially bolster our income during our golden years. And when my wife and I die, they inherit our residual income! No job I know of can ever provide that. I guess that's one reason why it's so satisfying to build this business. It's such a secure feeling to know that your work allows you to provide for all the members of your family even if you're no longer around. That's the kind of security I had in mind in the first place when I started my family. How about you?

Why Not Jump Right In?

Some of you may be thinking that you could increase your income faster if you would quit your job or sell your current business today and begin building your duplication business full-time. While that may sound like a great idea, the failure rate of those doing so is 90 percent, with the remaining 10 percent growing at a snail's pace. Why would that be the case? Doesn't it make sense that 100 percent of the effort put towards growing a business would make it stronger faster? Yes. On the surface this sounds good, but it's not. Here's why:

Most businesses that open up this year will be gone in less than two years. Why? There are many reasons but let's take a look at the major ones and how they relate.

What's the number one reason for business failure? Capital. Money. Moolah. Most businesses close because they run out of money. Many generate enough to keep the doors open but don't provide the income needed for family survival for things like food and shelter. When you keep your job or maintain your current business, while building this business, you can keep your income flow coming, provide food and shelter, and perhaps medical benefits to yourself and your family. Besides, this business requires no capital investment to get started and no inventory, no quotas, and no minimums to stay in business. So you can maintain your current standard of living as you build your residual income.

Another reason for business failure is often the lack of solid business knowledge on the part of the new owner. Once you purchase a business, it's a little late to figure out how it works and where all the potential problems are.

In this business you have someone to teach you what to do. They work with you at your pace, and for as long as you need them. They want to make sure you have a full understanding of every aspect you need to be successful. There are also books, tapes, videos, and seminars that can help you along the way. All of these tools are optional and you're never required to purchase or attend anything. It's totally up to you.

One other area that causes failure in many other businesses is staffing. If finances prevent you from hiring someone, you're truly the chief cook and bottle washer. What if you get sick? Who'll keep your business going? Or what if you want to do what you left the job market for—spend more time with your family?

In this business, you don't have to hire anyone. Remember, everyone who's a part of your business is also in their own independent business. They pay their own taxes and are responsible for their own business.

Diversification Gives You Freedom

Building this business at your own pace, while sustaining your present career, allows you to maintain a balanced life. You are not faced with the dilemma of who'll watch the store during an emergency or a family event. There is no store for people to come to; you conduct business from the privacy of your home, when you choose to.

Building this type of business also allows you the benefits of independence without the pitfalls of a conventional or franchise business. By diversifying through sharing this opportunity with others, who then get started in their own businesses, your income can multiply, giving you more time and money to enjoy life. If you need to limit or stop your activity for a period of time, for whatever reason, it doesn't stop the others you have helped from keeping things going. And remember, their businesses are a part of your business!

As the people you helped grow their businesses, yours grows too! Again, this is similar to what happens to a McDonald's Master Franchise. As income of the subfranchises grows, so does that of the master one, even though it physically doesn't do any more work than it did before! What could be better than that? The people in the proven support system that exists with this opportunity are there to help you—it's to their benefit! It's a win-win situation. And, you'll have someone who can teach you and help you regardless of how big or small you choose to build your business.

Chapter 6

Help Enough Others Get What They Want and You'll Have Everything You Want

*"When you are absolutely convinced of the possibility
and necessity of pursuing your dream, you take on a
different kind of driving energy. You add years to your life,
but more important, you add purpose and meaning to it."*
Les Brown

You May Be Asking, "What's in It for Me?"

When you're at work, why might you want to impress the boss? Would it be to get a promotion or a raise? Hey look, I understand. We all need to protect our primary source of income in order to provide for ourselves and our families.

But, what if each employee performed for the good of the company? If each person would go the extra mile and do more than is expected of them, it's likely the company would be more successful and everyone would earn more. I know that sounds like a fairy tale, but just imagine what would happen to any company if each worker did just that.

If that occurred, would we still have such a large number of layoffs? Would as many industries, that were once the foundation of our workforce, be downsizing or disappearing from the landscape? No! It's more likely they would become stronger and more profitable. Many of these companies would instead serve as shining examples of the type of success stories that inspire others to take action.

If you're in a supervisory or management position, what do you think would happen if you treated each employee as if they were going to be promoted to your job? How well do you think they would perform their current tasks? How loyal are they likely to be to you? If an emergency came up, would you be able to count on them to step up and produce or would they say, "It's not my job"? How many of them would continue the tradition and example you set and become better leaders for the company in the future?

Successful People Help Others—*That's the Key to Their Success!*

If you're employed by someone else, you've probably discovered by now that you can't control your boss. But, if you're fortunate enough to have quality leaders, learn from them and share that knowledge with those who are looking to you for leadership. That's the cornerstone of all success.

Truly successful people are successful for one primary reason: They committed their efforts to helping others get what they wanted. They took their focus from "What's in it for me?" and turned it into "How may I help you?" This simple but important attitude of focusing on the needs and wants of others is likely to have been the primary reason for their success. As they taught their associates this key idea, they may have found their income multiplying more quickly than expected. This attitude isn't altruistic; it's essential! Did you ever hear the expression, "You need to give before you receive"?

More importantly, they can now enjoy the fruits of their labors with friends rather than by themselves. Wouldn't you want to help your coworkers and friends achieve the success you enjoy so you're able to spend more time with them?

We could spend lots of pages discussing money, cars, homes, vacations, and whatever else you equate with success. But let me ask you something. Are you interested in providing more security for yourself and your family? Wouldn't you enjoy being able to have what you dreamed about when you got out of school or got married?

I don't know about you, but my wife and I got married to be together more. How about you? How would you feel about the opportunity to have more time for your children? When you help enough people achieve what they want, you will have what you want and more. You will enjoy a security that most people may have never even dreamed of. You will have financial peace of mind. And what's that worth?

Are you willing to invest 8 to 15 hours a week for the next two to five years to enjoy that kind of freedom? Are you willing to do more in order to provide more for those you love? If you're a parent, would you like to be home when the kids come home from school? Would you like to go on vacation, stay as long as you want, and not have a deadline to get back to work? By *investing* some of your time in this business every week, for the next two to five years, you could put yourself in a position to live the life you really want.

Delayed Gratification

I know you may be thinking, "I don't have the time." But the question is: "Will you ever have any time if you don't invest some now?" You've probably heard the expression that, "If you want more out of life you need to put more in." And as the old saying goes, "You need to give some of whatever you need more of." *The only difference between where you are now and where you want to be is what you do!* Keep in mind that you have all the time there is—we're all given 24 hours a day. You just don't know how much is left. None of us do.

There's hardly ever a perfect time to do anything. Just think about it. It's rarely convenient. The main thing is we need to *do something* that will lead us where we want to go if we ever honestly hope to get there. Just ask yourself these two questions: *If not this, what? If not now, when?*

To be, do, and have more we need to practice *delayed gratification.* Instead of having now and paying later, hold off. Work a little more now in order to have a lot more later. The cost of instant gratification may surprise you.

For example, assume you had a credit card charged to the limit of $3,000 at normal credit card rates, and you make only minimum payments. What would cause you to have such a debt? Perhaps a vacation that you really couldn't afford? A new giant screen TV? That's instant gratification paid back a little at a time.

How long does it take to pay that back? When I heard this answer, I was amazed. Thirty-one years! If you're a parent, imagine your children taking *their* children on vacations long before you've paid for the one you took them on.

What if you waited until you had the cash? At your current job, that may take a long time. But what if you were building a business that provided you with an extra $300, $500, or even $1,000 a month? How long would it take you to save for those extras? How much better would you feel about doing that without changing your current lifestyle? So what's the catch? You need to help others do just that using the system available to you. Is it worth it? What do you think?

How Can *You* Help Others Get Started?

Teach as you learn. The person who shared this book with you can help you learn what you need to know or they can introduce you to somebody else who can help you. They may be new at it too and not know much more than you do. Fortunately, they know successful people who can help you both. For example, one person who has helped me a lot in this business is a multi-millionaire. He travels the world with his wife, children, and grandchildren. Yet he's in my area of the country at least twice a month and I can have his help just for the asking. Guess how much it costs me? Zero— Zip—Nada!

He believes and practices the principles of this business and has been rewarded with more money and freedom than he ever imagined. Even while he's vacationing, his business continues to grow. Nevertheless, he's committed to the growth of the people he has shared this opportunity with.

His philosophy, which has become mine, is based on the idea that when you spend time helping others be successful, you can be more successful than you ever imagined. You can create a secure financial picture for your family and have friends you'd be happy to have your children know.

Bert and Terri Gulick—*Former Restaurant Owner and Clothing Store Manager*

When Bert and Terri became involved in this opportunity, they were both working two jobs. After spending up to 75 hours as a restaurant manager, Bert was putting in another 20 hours a week in a part-time job. Terri worked over 60 hours a week as a manager for a clothing store, and also had a job as a waitress.

One of the most common excuses people use NOT to get involved in this opportunity is lack of time. "But for us," Bert insists, "time was the *reason* to get involved…. We quickly realized the difference between working long and working smart!"

"We travel as a family," Terri says. "During the day we experience the sights and cultures of the world with our two girls. At night we help others build it so they can join us with their families."

"Gaining freedom for ourselves has been wonderful," states Bert, "but being able to share it with others is even more rewarding. Few things in life can compare to the feeling you get when you see the success of your associates. This is something that few businesses can offer."

Chapter 7
The Secret Is the System
*"All success is based on
following a system."*
John Fuhrman

The Strangest Question I've Ever Heard

When I was first introduced to this opportunity, I was asked a question that came from left field, or so I thought. The person said, "John, in two to five years, if money were no object, what would you like to be doing?" I couldn't think beyond my next paycheck, let alone that far down the road. I must have looked like a puppy. My head was tilted to one side in total ignorance. But his next question tied it all together.

"If you don't want anything more or different in your life, why would you be willing to do something different?" Then he asked me, "If you had more than enough money, would you pay off your car loan?" I replied, "Yes, and I'd be driving something else." "Would you still live in the house you're in now?" "No," I replied, "I'd live on the ocean." What he said next, though, *really* caught my attention.

He told me all of those things were possible but most people who only want those things (and don't believe they can have them) quit on themselves. No one will work extra for things they've been conditioned to believe they'll never have. What's the solution to this? We need to *believe* we can have our dreams—big or small. The *system* supports us in doing that.

He then asked me three questions. "Would you like to earn enough to have your wife become a full-time mom again?" "Would you like to be able to send your kids to the college of their choice without sacrificing your retirement?" And thirdly, "Would you like more security than you have now?" Needless to say, these questions made me think. As you may have guessed, I answered yes to all of them!

The Separation of Talkers and Doers

Then I was asked one final question. "Would you be willing to work an extra 8 to 15 hours a week for the next two to five years to provide yourself and your family with all we've talked about?"

For me there was only one answer. Then I asked lots of questions. Can I do it? Will I have help? What exactly do I have to do? You'll be getting some answers as you continue reading. But first, let me ask *you* a question.

Before you read any further, what would *you* be, do, and have in the next two to five years if time and money were no object? Write these things down on a piece of paper. Figure out as close as you can how much time and money you would need to accomplish all of your desires. You may be surprised.

Many people who have done this were happy to find out that they didn't need that much more time and money to have what they wanted. They just needed to eliminate some debt and unproductive activity, and have a continuous flow of extra income, and that would be enough.

How would you feel if, later in life, you found that things you thought impossible to attain were within your reach all along? Wouldn't it be sad if you had been given an opportunity to make these things happen and you mistakenly turned it down? What if you never even gave it a chance?

Now here's where the rubber meets the road. Would *you* be willing to work 8 to 15 hours a week for the next two to five years to get what you want? Remember, this is not a get rich quick scheme, something for nothing, or a guarantee of wealth. However, when anyone does more things that lead to success than the average person does, they'll have a better-than-average life. It's just that simple.

What Do You Have to Do?

Since you are in business for yourself, the answer is nothing. You can choose to do something or do nothing. It's totally up to you. If you do nothing, however, I can guarantee the results—no success with this business.

However, unlike most other businesses, you can become part of a system that'll teach you and help you stay motivated. There are people who can show you how to achieve what you want.

Like McDonald's and other successful franchises, this business has a proven system that has helped many people become successful. This system, too, has been fine-tuned over the years. It is taught by some of the top businesspeople throughout the world and is responsible for creating quite a number of the new millionaires over the last few decades. It no longer has to be proven. Its track record speaks for itself.

Two Kinds of Experts—*The Choice Is Yours*

If you were taught all about this business, even if you didn't have any experience, some folks may think you're an expert. Yet you're more likely to have financial success when you learn from the system as you go, perhaps failing on a daily basis until you understand what to do. Consider the following story:

Two boys begin a journey at the age of six. One reads everything he can get his hands on about the sport of swimming. He learns every record, commits each race to memory, and can remember who competed in every Olympic race since 1896.

The other boy begins practicing every morning. He loses almost as many races as he wins. His goal at each workout, race, and competition is to do the best he can without giving up. After 12 years of practice, the race of a lifetime begins. When it's over, an Olympic Gold Medal was hung around his neck. Both boys are experts while only one is a success. Which situation is more appealing to you?

You can spend your entire life gathering information about this or that opportunity. You can study the stories of those who have succeeded and analyze the failures of others. You can comment with authority, to the uneducated, how, based on your expertise, you would do things differently.

To be successful in any field you need to operate on faith and follow the example of those who have already succeeded. By doing this, you can avoid their mistakes and increase your growth. It's best to begin by putting your toe in the water and learn by doing. That's what I did.

Start as a student. You can then learn to teach and lead others—those who also have a strong desire to live their dream and are willing to do what it takes. This choice and your dedication can help you become a wealthy expert—one that the other experts will read about! It's just a decision away.

How to Shorten the Learning Curve

Start starting! Ask the person who shared this book with you how to approach people about their interest in doing more. You may be surprised how simple it is. Then go do it. We all had to start somewhere. If you wait until you're perfect at it, that day may never come. If you have even an inkling that this could be *the ticket* to achieving your dreams and a better life, why wait? Tell people you know first. They will understand you are new and may be interested in learning more just based on your enthusiasm.

As I discussed in one of my other books, *Reject Me—I Love It!—21 Secrets for Turning Rejection Into Direction,* having an idea rejected is actually an ideal event. You may discover you need to fine-tune your approach. That's to your benefit. If you sit around waiting for perfection, you'll be there for a long time—nothing or nobody is perfect. Just do the best you can with what you have when you have it.

Because of the mentors and teachers at your disposal, the fastest way to succeed is to discuss what you want to accomplish with those who have already done it. They can point out what you need to do in order to get where you want to be. The information they can provide is essential for you to succeed. Remember, in all likelihood, they have already made many of the common mistakes. They can watch you make the same ones or they can help you avoid them. The choice is yours. All you need to do is ask and they'll help you. Keep in mind, it's to their benefit to help you become successful as quickly as possible, so you both win.

Driving Toward Success—*A University on Wheels*

When you're on the road to and from work, doing errands, or on the way to visit family or friends, you could be getting the education of a lifetime. One aspect of the *support system* that's helped many people succeed is the continuing education program, which is optional. It includes audiocassette tapes which are available to you that can help you to be successful in the business—for a minimal cost, should you choose to take advantage of them. You can hear from those who have blazed the trail before you—those who have achieved their goals and dreams using this vehicle.

There are also tapes that tickle your funny bone and motivate you to move on. You may agree that those with the most impact give a message of hope from regular people just like you and me—people who wanted more out of life and became successful in this business. They give you the feeling of, *"If they can do it, so can I."*

New tapes are available every week. They're an inexpensive way to learn more and get and stay motivated. I have certain favorites that I listen to over and over. I also use some of them to introduce the concept to people to determine whether they have an interest or even if they qualify. You may want to ask the person who shared this book with you about the availability of such tapes. The time savings alone is worth it. The tapes work for you when you're not with the person who's listening to them!

There's a tape that addresses almost every situation imaginable. If you have a question you would like answered by someone successful in this business, a tape can often do it for you. How would you like to listen to a tape of a successful person who has done all that he or she talks about?

Remember, this University on Wheels is available for *you*. It's your choice whether or not you take advantage of the information the system offers. Purchasing these tapes is optional, depending on your needs and desires. There's no requirement to buy them. It's your business and your decision. But they are there when you want or need them.

Surround Yourself With Successful People

Whenever you decide to strive for a better life, you may have some family members, friends, and acquaintances who'll do everything they can to discourage you. Some do it under the pretense that they are looking out for your welfare. Frequently though, they're just jealous, pure and simple— which they're never likely to admit. You've probably experienced it before, maybe unknowingly, a time or two.

Some people may try to hold you back and tell you that what you're doing is only going to fill you with disappointment and cost you money. Deep down inside though, they probably wish they had the courage themselves to just go out and do something outside of the routines they've created in their lives.

Remember, anyone who has done anything out of the ordinary, frequently gets put down at first. After you've done what you've said you were going to do however, the naysayers generally come around. Imagine how people must have laughed at the Wright Brothers while they were developing the flying machine. But they didn't let that stop them!

When you find something you believe will help you and your family to have a better life, you'll need encouragement along the way. You'll find it makes a big difference when you associate with people who have been where you are and understand what you're going through. Each month, all over the world, there are optional seminars that allow you to do just that. In fact, there may be one within a few minutes of where you live.

At these seminars you can learn from people who live in your area who have become successful in this business. They'll share experiences and information that can help you achieve your dreams more quickly. The economic climate where they live is likely to be similar to yours. And your results could be as good or even better, when you listen and apply what you've learned. Another benefit is that you'll be surrounded by people who not only understand your situation, but will also encourage you every step of the way. Again, it's up to you what you choose to do.

The Secret to Your Success

As mentioned earlier, some of you may agree that McDonald's does not make the best hamburgers. Nevertheless, they sell more every day than most restaurants could ever hope to sell in a hundred lifetimes! Why? They have a system, and so do we.

The first part of our system is education and motivation through books, tapes, and seminars. Using the example and techniques of those who have already succeeded can help you get where you're going sooner. They'll also share what they did that didn't work so you can avoid repeating their mistakes.

When you follow a proven pattern of success, fine-tuning your skills along the line, it is extremely *difficult not to succeed*. In fact, the only way to fail is to quit! After more than three years of being in this business the only changes in my family and myself have been for the better, and the only lessons I've learned have been from watching, listening, and doing. I've found the secret—it's *the system*.

Those of us who are students of the system are very fortunate, indeed. It's not for everybody; but it is the ticket to a better life for a lot of us. Since it's your future we're talking about, you need to do what you believe is best for you. It's your decision.

The Short Story of Two Former Teachers—*Rick and Sue Lynn Setzer*

From their appearance on the covers of fine magazines like *The Robb Report,* it's very inspiring to learn that Rick and Sue Lynn were former teachers. Fortunately, someone thought enough of them to show them this business. Says Rick, "I was afraid NOT to get in for fear it might work!"

A short time later, Rick and Sue Lynn caught fire. In the beginning there were only a few instructional tapes available. Rick invested in all of them and as a result of the tapes and hard work, they added over 1,000 people to their business.

Many of those people have gone on to great success and wealth. They simply followed the path created by the system and their leaders. Do what the people are doing who are where you want to be and the rewards can be yours too.

Chapter 8

Do You Believe You Don't Know Anyone?

*"Everybody knows at least 250 people
and is only, at most, seven people away
from contacting anyone."*
Author Unknown

I Didn't Believe I Knew Anyone Either

Other than not having time, saying they don't know anyone is the most common reason people have for not taking advantage of this opportunity. I understand. So how could I possibly understand that you may be feeling that way when we've never met? I know because I've been there.

The first time someone shared this opportunity with me, it made a lot of sense. I just didn't believe I knew anyone. Fortunately, my wife had the nerve to call someone I "didn't know"—*one of my brothers!*

What Could We Be Afraid Of?

It's not that we're afraid of telling people about things that could help them. If that's not it, why would we be afraid? Our fear is likely to be that we might not be able to handle their response. Let me clear the mystery up right now. Some people may tell you no because they don't think it will work for *them.*

This is curious because 70 percent of the U.S. population is dissatisfied with their job or standard of living. Most people would like to improve their lives but they don't realize there's something they could do without taking a financial risk. Many folks have also been led to believe they're secure. Yet, at the same time, all of the corporate downsizing is scaring them. As you know, some people are, of course, legitimately comfortable and happy with the way things are.

Because we don't like to be rejected, or maybe we're so desperate to be accepted, we may not want to rock the boat. We may want to wait to show how excited we are until others get excited too. The trouble with that approach is, how can others get enthused unless we share the opportunity?

Consider this: As people get older, you may often hear them say, "If only...." (fill in the blank) about something or some time. Have you ever heard, "If only I had bought that land back in 19--"? Had they known about a certain stock when it first became available, they'd be set for life. They don't consider the fact that the people who bought such stock, land, or something else that's now valuable, took a chance when they purchased it. It's true they may now be wealthy, but it wasn't just luck. They *took action*. Nothing much happens without taking action.

The person who bought the first McDonald's may have gotten laughed at, but he didn't let that stop him. I would imagine that McDonald's pioneer families now laugh all the way to the bank. These days only already successful people can afford one! You now have that kind of opportunity with the same safeguards—a proven system, a huge support team, and virtually no downside risk. Surely, there's someone you could share this opportunity with. And the key word is *share*.

Even if you're a master salesperson, you can't successfully sell this business. *All you can really do is find out what people want, share the business and all its benefits, and have it either accepted or rejected.* I can tell you as a career salesperson and sales trainer, everybody that I *sold* this to, quit. Those who took it at face value and on faith, because they wanted to achieve their dream, are moving in the right direction. They're getting closer and closer to their dreams and goals every day.

Who Would You Share It With First?

Get a blank piece of paper and a pen. If I told you that the next ten people you shared this opportunity with would want to join you, who would you want to talk to? If you've already started a list, great. If not, make a list of these ten people and more. In fact, write down as many names as you can think of. Find out how to approach these folks from the person who shared this book with you.

If the people on your list aren't looking right now, that's fine. The timing for them may not be right, or they may just be headed in another direction.

Build Relationships and Build a Business—*The Key to All Success*

In any successful endeavor, there's always at least one person, or a group of people who are respected and trusted by those who joined them to build the enterprise. It's the same way in this business. It's important to have mutual respect and trust with those you want to associate with.

To accomplish that, you need to build relationships with people first, then you can potentially build a business together. *All businesses, regardless of the industry, are created by building relationships.* People want to do business with people who are interested in them.

Show an interest in others. Find out what their dreams are and determine how serious they are about them. How much are they willing to work for them? Offer to match their effort to help them achieve their goals. When they realize your main focus is on helping them succeed, you may be amazed at how quickly your business can grow. *People don't care how much you know until they know how much you care.*

You're likely to have a more positive attitude as you build this business. It's easier to be self-confident when you're excited about your future and focused on helping others achieve a better life. You'll also learn how to adjust your attitude, if necessary.

Having a positive attitude is contagious. The people you deal with on a regular basis are likely to notice your new sparkle. They may even ask why you seem to be so happy lately. Just tell them that the more they pursue their dreams, while helping others achieve theirs, the happier they'll be too.

It is such a gratifying experience to be a part of the success of others—to see them come alive with renewed hope. There's nothing like it. As professional speaker and success trainer Zig Ziglar says, *"When you help enough other people get what they want, you'll get what you want."*

What's the Best Way to Start?

Since it seems that you have the desire and ambition to be, do, and have more, this book could help you open the door to achieving your dreams. You may be so excited about the possibilities that, all of a sudden, trying to come up with people to share this with may seem difficult. That's okay. You just need to approach it a bit differently, that's all.

The solution is to take a deep breath and relax. Write down the names of the last six people you've enjoyed having at your house for socializing or some other fun activity. How about those you may have gone out to dinner or someplace else with. Picture having the freedom to be with them most any time you want to, doing anything together that strikes your fancy.

You can learn how to approach these people and others from the person who shared this book with you or one of their associates. Some of your friends may tell you they're not interested. That's okay. They're probably just not looking for an opportunity at this time.

Regardless of their answer, remember, they're still friends. Always leave the door open for later. Don't shut them off just because they don't want to move on like you do. There could be circumstances that you're unaware of that make this the wrong time for them. Respect their position and maintain their friendship. They may change their mind later or when they see you succeed. It's up to them. After all, you have friends who don't work where you do, don't you? You're still friends, even though you have different lifestyles and jobs. And it's unlikely that you agree on everything. Right? So go ahead and follow your dream. After all, who knows? When you start achieving more in your life, they may even call you! It does happen. People like to be around winners.

You May Have Run Out of People! *Now What?*

There are about 275 million people in the U.S. alone, as mentioned earlier, and over 6 billion in the world! Don't you think that over the next few years you just might meet a few more of them? What if some of them turned out to be interesting, motivated people who you would enjoy spending more time with? And what if they *are* looking?

When you take an interest in others, you can make new friends, and friends share opportunities with friends. When you build relationships and help people get what they want, you can build a secure financial future and truly have what *you* want.

Chapter 9
Dreambuilding Is the Key

*"Into each life comes a time to grow
when dreams must be spoken and wings
must be tried...so reach for your dreams,
spread your new wings...and fly."*
John Fuhrman

Nothing Happens Without a Dream!

In my seminars throughout the world and in the book *Reject Me—I Love It!*, I discuss the difference between how and why. It's the difference between complacently settling for a life that you're no longer excited about or picturing the outcomes you want and moving toward them. Knowing how to do something isn't enough.

You need to have a big enough *reason WHY* to drive you to the finish line. It's the key to all success. *You need to have a dream.*

I know it may sound corny, but consider this: Millions of little boys play baseball every summer. But how many make it to even the Minor Leagues? As you may have guessed, not many. Of that small number, only a few ever get to stand for the national anthem as a player in one of 28 Major League ballparks. What do you suppose the difference is between Little League players and those of the Major Leagues? Is it possible that one person is 1,000 times better than another? Can you really know 1,000 times more about the game? The answer to both questions is no.

Ray Kroc, Sam Walton, J. Paul Getty, and Andrew Carnegie were all wealthy beyond most people's ability to comprehend. Did they work a million times more hours than you do? Did they attend a million times better school? Are they a million times more skilled than you? Again, the answers are no. There is *something*, though, that *does* separate them from most people. It seems like there's a million miles between them and the majority of folks. But in reality, they took one key step that most people miss. And that made all the difference.

Those that make it to the top are simply people of *vision*. They have a *dream*. That is where vision comes from. These people see themselves where they want to be rather than where they are. They become passionate about getting to a destination and are willing to do what it takes to get there. *The difference between dreaming and not is like the difference between an escalator and a treadmill.* You may work up a sweat on a treadmill, but it won't take you anywhere.

Dreams and Wishes—*Any Difference?*

You can do anything you set your mind to. Did you ever hear that? Do you believe it? Unfortunately, not many do. So what is a dream? It's something we'd love to accomplish. Something we have become passionate about being, doing, or having. We have a focus so sharp, we can actually picture it happening.

The instant we set a target date for making it come true, the dream becomes a goal.

Wanting to win the lottery, hoping for the best, saying, "Maybe someday I'll…," and things like that, are simply wishes. True dreams can and do happen to those who stick to their commitment to follow through. For instance, I have already pictured this book in the hands of readers all over the world. I just knew in my heart, it would make a major difference in the lives of others. Therefore, I became committed to its completion. Once that took place, once I became committed and focused on the completion of the dream—I had done the most difficult part; making the decision! Creating and typing the manuscript page by page was actually the easiest part! Deciding is half done.

When someone offers you something that could change your life for the better, how do you see it? Those who truly want to experience such a change, see the opportunity; those who are complacent often find it too good to be true. Those honestly seeking a better life, see the dream; those wallowing in the status quo—unhappy, but unwilling to do anything about it—see it as a wish that would be nice if it came true.

That's how this business is. Those who aren't willing to just settle for can drive this financial vehicle to wherever they want to go. Those who choose to just accept things as they are will see nothing and get exactly that. Those who dream are more likely to see this opportunity as a tool for them to use to get what they want.

Those who only wish they had a better life and wonder why they don't, are likely to ask, "If it's so good, how come everyone isn't doing it?" Those who dare will spread their wings like an eagle and soar above the crowd. Those who are complacent will move aside as you pass, and wonder what happened.

How Do I Build My Dream?

Every now and then, when you may be feeling, "There's got to be more to life than this," you may start picturing how you'd like it to be. Maybe you're driving a beautiful new sports car, or perhaps you're on a nice long vacation playing golf, or doing something else you love to do. It may even be as simple as being at home with your kids when other parents have to go to work. It doesn't matter. Whatever it was, it vanished from your mind.

But what if you could put it back? Bring it into sharper focus. Even get so detailed, it almost seems real. Is it really possible your dreams could come true? *Absolutely!*

Your mind will never imagine something unless you are capable of achieving it! Did you know that? That's why you probably never found the cure for any disease, or invented a better mouse trap. But to avoid getting down on yourself, believe this: *"Whatever the mind can conceive and believe, it can achieve."* Napoleon Hill shares that observation in his bestselling book *Think and Grow Rich.* It's a compilation of his 20 years researching the wealthy people of the world. He found the secret to wealth by studying the wealthy. We are fortunate in this business to associate with and learn from wealthy people who also share their success secrets with us.

Find the one dream that gets you the most excited and write it down. Now detail it to the max. Keep making it more specific and more definite. Dreaming for a lot of money just won't work. That's just a wish. You can however, dream that you will have saved $50,000 or more. That's a dream. But it's only the beginning. You need to get specific. Set a goal. By what date will you have it? What is it for? What are you willing to do to get it? Will the money come all at once or a little at a time? These are just examples of questions that you need to ask yourself to make your dream crisp and vividly real in your mind.

Once you have the specifics figured out, you can focus on the steps you need to take, one day at a time, toward your dream. In the beginning there may be little or no results. At first you will work and work and work and nothing may seem to be happening. Understand though, that getting things in motion toward your dream and acquiring momentum takes the most energy. It's like the space shuttle—95 percent of the fuel is used just to launch the rocket and get it into orbit. The remaining 5 percent takes care of the rest of the mission. In fact, once it's in orbit, its momentum keeps it going with no further expenditure of fuel required. The only time any fuel is consumed is during maneuvering and course corrections.

Working toward your dream is similar. Once you have the momentum established, it's easier to keep going and attract more people.

As you persist, a glimmer of your dream will appear. When you follow the principles outlined in this book, others will begin to help you make your dream come true. And the closer you get to realizing your dream, the easier it's likely to become. There *is* light at the end of the tunnel. Have confidence that you're doing the right thing and that it will happen.

The Potato Chip Factor

If I offered you a big bag of potato chips to eat and asked you to eat them all right now, many of you would turn it down because it's just too much. However, if I just gave you one chip and said that's all you can have today, a lot of you would soon want the whole bag. In fact, you may even plan a way to get it. Dreams are like that.

Suppose you've mentally pictured your dream home, like many people have. Then one day you see a house listed in the newspaper that's almost exactly like it. The best thing you can do is make an appointment to go see it or perhaps attend an open house. Once you get a taste of how it would be to live there, tell yourself, "Not today, but I'll be back." As you leave, your mind begins working on ways to get you back inside to take another look. First, only for a few more minutes, but then you dream of living there permanently. Now you have increased your belief.

Your dream becomes a passion. Soon, you want to put energy into getting it. You may begin to realize that you need to do something in addition to your current job or business to have your dream come true. You now have more of a reason to invest some time and effort, outside of your present career, to create additional income. You're looking forward to a brighter future, and life becomes more exciting for you!

When you have a purpose in mind, it's much easier doing what you need to do. Focusing on what you *really* want to accomplish helps you get through the challenges along the way. You need a vision. You need to *build a dream—your dream!*

What if You Don't Have a Dream?

We can help you discover your dream. It's an important part of being successful. Without a dream to protect and motivate us, some of us would float from one excuse to the next. Without a dream, each night becomes "not tonight." Without a dream, we may think all other successful people are materialistic. Without a dream, we may settle for just getting by. Without a dream most people say "someday," which turns into a new word called never.

Having a dream is a large part of what makes all great and successful people tick. They follow their dream. It's also one of the key ingredients of being happy, as is having more control of your life and your destiny. We're all born with a free will, but it's up to us to use it. You can do virtually anything you really, really want to do as long as you have a big enough dream.

GUIDELINES FOR MAKING YOUR DREAMS COME TRUE

+ **D**ecide what you want and passionately go for it!
+ **R**each for the "impossible" and be humble when you achieve it.
+ **E**xpect help from no one and be amazed at all the helping hands.

- ◆ **A**llow for mistakes, accept them, learn from them, and move on.
- ◆ **M**ake every move be toward your dream and each step will bring you closer.
- ◆ **S**top at nothing in your quest to achieving your dreams.

Beginning today, those of you who are serious about your future need to commit to getting the most out of life, or it's likely you'll just get by. Stop settling for and begin shooting for the stars. The only thing keeping you from what you deserve is you. Decide what it is you want, find a vehicle that will take you there, and, in Nike's famous words, *"Just Do It!"*

Chapter 10

Contrary to What Your Mother May Have Said, Always Talk to Strangers

*"Show a sincere interest in others.
Strangers are but unmet friends."*
Author Unknown

Now What?

You've gotten excited about your dream and you may be starting to take the steps to begin building your business. Perhaps every acquaintance, relative, and friend on your list has been called. That may have taken all of about two weeks. Some of them may still be laughing at you for trying to improve your life, while others may be jealous. Some may even be secretly interested but they're not about to admit it.

Even though some people you know may not be interested, *you* may see this business as the opportunity of a lifetime as many others do. You may really want to build it so you can live your dream.

It just doesn't matter what other people may think, say, or do. That's just where they are and it's totally their business. *Remember, anybody who ever did anything out of the ordinary was put down by at least one person and probably many more.* The naysayers and critics are often there, ready to tear you down. But there are no statues erected in their honor, and they don't know what it's like to live your life. You're the decision maker in your life!

The question you may be asking yourself now is, "Who do I talk to once I've talked to everyone I know?" Well, you could share this business concept with total strangers and play the odds. When you share it with enough people, sooner or later you'll run into someone who's interested. Or, you can do what we're now talking about—meeting new people and building relationships. Then, if there's an interest, you could share this opportunity.

More questions may now be pouring into your mind. "How can I share it with a stranger? When should I spring this on them?"

The answer to the second question is *never*. Never spring anything on anyone. This is an opportunity for you to help those who are willing to work for the results they want. Springing something on someone comes across like a trap and puts them on the defensive. The last thing you want to do is trap someone into something. Under those circumstances, both of you will certainly fail.

The answer to the first question is never share anything with a stranger! Now you may be wondering, "So, what can I do?" Fortunately, life and its answers are often quite simple. We're the ones who normally complicate things. *Before you share anything with someone new, the best thing you can do is simply to first make a friend.* You might start by just saying, "Hi, how's it going?" If they so much as acknowledge your presence, congratulations, you're on your way. The progression of this contact is a bit more involved but many people overcomplicate this step and quit before they start. Basically, you want to start a new friendship. After all, all of your current friends were once strangers! All relationships begin with strangers.

Perhaps this scenario would fit in your local area. I'll be the person starting the relationship as I enter a store and meet the person behind the counter. For simplicity we'll call him New Friend and I'm John. You can use your own name!

John: Hi, how's it going?

New Friend: Not too bad.

John: Is this your store?

New Friend: No, I just work here.

John: This looks like a great store. I'll bet they pay you well.

New Friend: Are you kidding? I just barely get by.

John: You plan on working here the rest of your life?

New Friend: I'm out of here the second something better comes along.

John: Say, I do some traveling in my business. Perhaps I'll run into something along the way. What is it you'd like to do?

New Friend: A good job with a steady income.

John: How much would you like to make?

New Friend: $50,000.

John: If you made that kind of money, how would your life be different?

New Friend: I'd take better vacations.

John: Where would you go?

New Friend: I'd like to take the kids to DisneyWorld.

John: That's great. Hey listen. If I come across something like you're talking about, would you like me to give you a call?

New Friend: Absolutely!

John: Look, I can't promise you anything. But if you write down your name and number I'll call you if something comes up. If I don't call you in a couple of weeks, feel free to give me a call. Here's my card.

Done. That whole process takes less than three minutes. I can guarantee one thing: If that person is seriously looking for an opportunity, they'll be waiting by the phone for your call. However, I wouldn't call them for at least two weeks. Otherwise you'll appear like an anxious salesperson. And nobody wants to be sold. When you show them that you're sincerely interested in helping them find the right opportunity for them, they'll look forward to learning more about what you have.

Make a Friend a Day

Setting a goal of talking to one new person a day will not only help you build your business, but also help you develop new friendships that could last a lifetime. After all, you can never have too many friends! Remember though, friends who don't choose to do what you do can still be your friends. Some may join you in the business. However, don't put your life on hold waiting for them to go out, meet people, and make more friends. They may not have as big a dream as you do.

It's important to continue building relationships, but don't chase people. (Remember the pigeons in the park.) Share this opportunity because you sincerely believe it will better their lives, not just because there's something in it for you. Be other-centered. Do what's best for others and you'll both win!

Consistently creating new friendships and sharing this opportunity with the ones who are interested, is key to having constant growth in your business. This is because you can put people into three basic groups: now, not right now, and never. Some of the people you share this opportunity with will be excited and want to get started immediately. Others never do anything right away; they may want to check you and it out more thoroughly, and perhaps even see how well you do, before they make a decision. Finally there are those who will, flat out, say no. In some cases, no matter what you offered them opportunity-wise, they'd still say no. They're just not looking.

Meeting someone new every day increases your chances of getting more yeses. You are constantly planting seeds—meeting people, some of whom may lead to a bountiful harvest.

Since some of the people will say yes immediately, they're easier to deal with; so let's talk about the others. The people who honestly think about it before they make a decision may be your best candidates. When they do say yes they generally become the most loyal, since they've convinced themselves. And they're often the ones who surprise you with their yes after somebody else told you no!

Here's something you can do more easily, even if you feel a little shy when you talk to someone for the first time. After the initial exchange, don't ask about them. Just ask if they know anybody. Here's how:

John: Hello, how's it going?
New Friend: Pretty good.
John: This is a great store. Are you the owner?
New Friend: No, I just work here.
John: Do you live around here?
New Friend: All my life.
John: I'm considering expanding a business in the area and I'm looking for a few key people. Do you know of anyone who is sharp and ambitious and looking for an opportunity?

This conversation can take several directions, but the point is, you were indirect. This way your new friend isn't likely to feel they've been put on the spot. Therefore, they may actually feel you're leaving them out, and may be inclined to ask you, "What about me?" And you could then reply, "Look, I can't promise you anything. But if you'll write your name and number down, perhaps I'll give you a call the next time I'm in the area. Maybe we could get together and have a cup of coffee."

This way, *he* actually invited *you* to contact *him!* You didn't chase him! Rather you pushed him back by planting doubt in his mind that you would, indeed, call him. People want what they don't think they can have! You care about him as a person and what's best for him, but the fact is, you're only looking for somebody who actually wants to do something. Your time is too valuable to play games.

The new friend could also say, "You need to talk to Joe Jones. He's real smart and he's always looking to make more money." I recommend you still get the new friend's name and number so when you call Joe you can say, "I was speaking with so-and-so last week about expanding a business in your area and he suggested I call you. Look, I can't promise you anything, but I'll be in the area next week. I'm quite busy and I don't have a whole lot of time. My schedule is fairly tight right now, but if you're serious, perhaps we could get together for a cup of coffee and explore the possibilities."

Again, you're pushing him back. You're placing a value on what you have to offer and your time; you're being exclusive in your presentation. This is called posturizing.

In the last example you're letting the person lead you exactly where you want to go. You want to perk *their* interest by your indirect approach, if possible. You're also looking for others they may know of who may be interested. There's a possibility you could achieve either or both of these things. Then again, you may generate no interest at all. All you can do is give it your best shot. After that, it's up to them.

Understand, once you're convinced that this opportunity is right for you and believe, as many do, that you have the best thing going, those who aren't interested won't matter to you. You're only looking for someone who really wants to do something. You're much better off with a few eager beavers than with a bunch of lazy people who really don't want to do anything; they would only sap your energy.

Many people find it's easier to talk to strangers than people they know. For one thing, people you don't know don't have a preconceived idea about you, your desires, or your success track record. Also, if such people aren't that interested in what you have to offer, you're unlikely to ever see them again. More importantly, there are many more people in this world who you don't know than the number of people you do know. You have a better selection of people to choose from.

When you think of it, it's similar to many other industries who are creating new business relationships to expand their operations! Most successful business people are constantly looking for new people to do business with. For instance, has a local merchant or salesperson been friendly enough with you that you'd be interested in building a relationship with them?

The more people you share this opportunity with, the more success you're likely to have. While it's fine to share with family, friends, and acquaintances, it's also important to talk to strangers, and turn them into friends. With those who choose to come along, you could build a bigger business than you ever thought possible. That's what all successful businesspeople do.

Chapter 11
Your Friends May Not Understand

"Most people who you believe are thinking about you, probably aren't. They're too busy thinking about themselves. So, you might as well do what you want to do."
John Fuhrman

What's This Business Really About?

By now, you may be wondering what this business is all about. In a nutshell, it's about you and your dreams. As the title asks, "Are You Living Your Dream?" That's important to you, right? If so, hang in there.

In upcoming chapters, we'll discuss some of the actual mechanics of this business. And you'll get a better understanding of how it works. You may have come this far on faith and hope. Part of you may believe this could be exactly what you're looking for and the other part of you might simply hope it is. In business (and in general) that's called attitude, which will account for 90 percent of your success. The other 10 percent is knowledge and technique.

Your Friends May Try to Protect You

Your friends are likely to respond more favorably to your attitude than to your knowledge about the business. Why? Simply because they're your friends. They know that a week or so ago you were just one of the gang and you couldn't possibly have become an expert at a business so quickly. The details you offer may cause them to question and be skeptical, just like you may have been! They may automatically try to *protect you from yourself* by discouraging you. Think about it. Here are people you've known for years who may be telling you this idea of yours can't possibly work. Who are you going to believe—the person sharing this book with you, or those who don't know what you know?

So What's This Dream Stuff Anyway?

Have you wondered why I haven't discussed many of the details of this business—even though you're more than halfway through the book? It's because they're not as nearly important as your dream. If you opened this book and were flooded with details, you may not have even gotten through the first chapter. The most important thing you really need to know is *why* you want to build it. This business is just a vehicle you can use to achieve your dreams and goals.

How Might Your Friends React?

Do you realize your friends may question facts, but probably not your enthusiasm? If you bury them with facts and figures, they may ask you to defend them. They may also want to know how *you're* doing. When you say you're just starting, they'll probably ask you how you know it works. They may try to put you on the defensive—but you don't need to defend the fact that you want more out of life. That's a personal choice. Remember, everyone is most interested in themselves and what you're doing is probably not at the top of their agenda. Whatever the case may be, *a true friend will always encourage you.*

Another reason some of your friends may try to discourage you is because they don't want you to move ahead of them! That's okay. Let them be. We all choose how we live our own lives. An interesting thing may happen, however. As you become more successful, some of your friends may join you. Besides, you'll also make a lot of new friends.

Some of your friends may get in this business and some may not. Just because you may be ready to move on, doesn't necessarily mean they are. Some will simply support you from the sidelines. Keep in mind, many of your friends and acquaintances have jobs and careers that are different from yours. And you're still friends, right? I have friends who are not in this business. But I've made many more new friends because of this business. The good news is, you can have it both ways.

Help Your Friends Dream

Instead of trying to convince them of something they might not understand, why not talk about something they do? Simply say to them things like: "Picture us being able to go on vacations together with no time limit or deadlines; Imagine being able to do all the things we've talked about doing but we haven't done like ____; Imagine us working together toward a common goal without the pressures of a boss." These are the things I understood when a friend showed me the business. I could relate to that a lot more than a bunch of numbers. Maybe your friends are the same way.

Encourage your friends and acquaintances to dream. Let them know you, and the people supporting you, are willing to help *them* achieve *their* dreams and get *them* to where *they* want to be. It'll be different for each of them. Some will only need a little support, as they take the business and run with it. However, others may need more help. The flexibility of this business will allow you, and the people helping you, to do whatever the person needs. The benefit for you is that each person you help to succeed brings you closer to your goals and dreams!

Chapter 12
This Sounds Good, But...
*"One's mind, once stretched by a new idea,
never regains its original dimensions."*
Oliver Wendell Holmes

Is This Really a Good Opportunity?

We are often judged by the company we keep. Remember in your youth when your parents were constantly telling you who not to associate with? Any long-term association becomes, to some degree, a blend of the thinking and behavior of the associates. If you hang around with lazy people, you may become lazy too. On the other hand, when you associate with people more successful than you are, you can achieve more success in your own life as you duplicate their winning habits. It just rubs off, as they say.

In this business you can associate with some of the world's most respected companies—General Motors, Visa, Panasonic, Ford, Seiko, MCI, and over 1,500 other name-brand companies. Because of the great success these companies have had in doing business with us, more are trying to do so every week. These companies have more lawyers and accountants to check us out than most of us could imagine. I figured that, since this business is good enough for them to supply their products and services, it was at least worth my consideration.

I was asked three questions that really made me think: "If not *this*, then what?" "If not *now*, then when?" "What else is out there that *even comes close*?" You might want to ask yourself these same things. How would *you* answer these questions?

This Business Practices What It Preaches

Earlier, we discussed the importance of income diversification. *Putting all your eggs in more than one basket is essential for financial survival and success.* If one investment or income-producing aspect of your finances underperforms, the rest will see you through.

Today, there are a number of opportunities available to generate extra income. You may have been approached by people doing some of them. Unfortunately, many are missing the big picture. They may have only one product or service, or perhaps a limited number, making it difficult to diversify.

This opportunity does everything it teaches you to do. The product line is diversified enough that you could specialize if you wanted to, in almost any area, and still create a great secondary or primary income. (Although this is an option, I recommend that you and those you associate with avail yourselves of everything that the system offers, rather than having a singular focus.)

How diversified is it? To put it simply, the companies who supply goods and services to our duplication system can provide you with almost everything you need!

Our corporate supplier also provides its own 100 percent satisfaction guarantee on virtually everything it offers. Even if the manufacturer doesn't guarantee it beyond a short period, they do in almost every case. On many major appliances they even double the warranty from the factory.

Discounts and Tax Benefits—*But Not Quotas*

Because of the size of this business, the buying power is already established. This allows you to purchase all your products at wholesale or discounted rates. Furthermore, you have no inventory requirements. You buy only what you personally need, when you need it. It's likely you'll be spending less on the goods and services you're currently using. And instead of going to the store, *you are, in effect, the store*—without a storefront or inventory! Keep purchasing your personal and home-care items, cereal, snacks, clothes, vitamins, food supplements, household items, and such, as you always have. *But instead of going to the store and giving them the profit, buy all these things "from yourself" and save time and money.*

All this means no investment in equipment, or a garage full of products to get stuck with. All you need to get started (depending on what country you're in) is around $150. This includes about $90 worth of products, $60 worth of educational materials, and an application. And it's all satisfaction guaranteed, or your money back.

The only other thing you need to consider now is your commitment. Understand, this is *your* business. You can do as little or as much as you want. However, what you get out of it will depend on what you put in to it. Once you get started, there's nothing you're required to do or spend. Your income depends on you. If you do nothing, it will be easy to estimate your income—zero!

Any commitment you make will be based on what you think you can get out of it. If you're honestly looking to generate some strong additional income, you need to treat this business seriously. While the around $150 you invest is small in terms of starting a business, don't think for a minute that this is a small business. In fact, this business has done over $7 billion in one year and it keeps on growing.

If you inventoried all the products, hired the shipping people, administered the bonus programs, and erected the buildings to do all this, you'd invest millions. Fortunately, the *system* makes none of that necessary on your part. It's already done. This allows you to do your business from your home! And, in addition, you'll have business tax benefits that you don't have now if you're working for someone else.

Check It Out

Once you've finished this book and learned the rest of the details from the person who shared it with you, you can still get more information before coming aboard if you're still not sure about what to do. As a matter of fact, it's likely to be recommended that you don't invest any money at all until you're absolutely sure this will work.

When you understand the logic, common sense, and people behind this business, you'll know the system works. The real questions for you may be, "Will it work for *me*? Can *I* do it?"

Before you get started, talk to others who are already successfully doing it. This business has people coming together from all over the world. Also ask about the successful people who have followed the system and have become millionaires. Find out about their backgrounds. Can you relate to their backgrounds and where they came from?

What's the Catch?

There is no free lunch—no guarantee of success. Again if you're looking for a get rich quick scheme, this isn't it. I don't believe there is such a thing. No one can promise you anything. Base your decision on the facts and how serious you are about living your dream. Or maybe you just want to increase your income to ease your monthly financial situation. That's fine. It's up to you to determine what *you'd* like to do.

Whatever you decide, remember this. You're now aware of a vehicle that can help you eliminate your financial concerns and help you make your dreams come true.

The big catch is, this could be one of the most important issues you've ever had to deal with. It may be the first time in your life that you finally realize your future is totally up to you. You decide whether or not to move on. Nobody else is in your shoes. Nobody else pays your bills or has your dreams. You're the only one who can say yes for yourself.

Your future is in your hands. Regardless of your decision, the consequences or the rewards are yours.

You can be well rewarded for your efforts. If they're minimal, your income will reflect that. When you share this with enough other people, however, everything you ever dreamed of can come true. As one of the children who starred in the Disney movie, *Angels in the Outfield* said, "It could happen."

Chapter 13
Your Friends Don't Pay Your Bills

"If man does not keep pace with his companions, perhaps it is because he hears a different drummer. Let him skip to the music he hears, however measured and far away."
Henry David Thoreau

Consider the Source

There aren't many guarantees in life, but whenever someone does something to better themselves, you can guarantee certain responses.

When I first got started, some of my friends ran to my side to protect me. They told me I would be wasting my time and these things never worked. They were relentless and believed they were saving me from ruin. Some of them were co-workers with many more years in the business world than I had and I *almost* listened to them.

Then I thought about my future. I looked at those who had been working in my profession five years more than I had. I figured if I continued to work at my job five more years, I would then be where they are.

If you don't think you have it so bad, look at someone who's been working a job like yours five years longer than you have. Ask yourself, *"Is that where I want to be?"* and *"Will I be satisfied when I get there?"* I didn't like what I saw. And, since those people didn't seem to be doing anything to change where they were, I concluded they had *no right* to tell *me* what to do.

The other type of person you'll be guaranteed to run into is what I call the anything person. They try anything that comes along that looks easy. At the first sign of work, they quit and move on to the next thing. They'll get right in your face and tell you, with authority, this won't work. If you needed brain surgery, would you want a specialist or someone who failed med school and told you it didn't work?

There are lots of success stories in this business. Because it is a multi-billion-dollar business and growing virtually everywhere in the world, some of these people may live in your hometown or nearby. I suggest you get back with the person who shared this book with you and ask them if you could meet some of the successful people in this business. One of the great things about this system is that you can get the help you need to enjoy the same success they have.

You're Breaking the Circle

It's important to consider some things when it comes to your friends. Some of your friendships may be long-term. They may do a lot to protect the friendship—to keep it the same as it was. Birds of a feather really do flock together and that certainly holds true in friendship. You are friends because of similar likes, income levels, and such. You've had something in common bonding you together.

As you become more successful and increase your income, you might choose to move to a better neighborhood, take different vacations, travel in different circles, or make other changes that some of your friends may not. Did the friends you had in first grade follow your path in life? Probably not. It's likely your interests and careers have taken you in different directions. That's life.

Unlike another job, however, which requires different associations and perhaps relocation, this opportunity allows you to take your friends along, right where you're living now. You don't need to move and you can also make new acquaintances and friends on your own terms.

If your current friends and acquaintances choose not to move on with this opportunity, that's simply their choice. That doesn't mean you still can't be friends. I have friends who aren't in this business, but they do whatever they can to support me and my efforts and I do the same for them. It's called mutual respect. Each of you is doing what you feel is best for you and your family. You can still support each other, even though you may never work together.

The bottom line is, you need to do what you believe is best for you and your family. Would you like some help with your current financial situation? Do you want to improve your lifestyle? Maybe you're happy where you are and have already achieved some or all your dreams. Then again, like many others, you may want to move on. All of us need to provide security and create a lifestyle as we see fit. In any case, since your friends don't pay your bills, it's up to you to explore any avenue that can do just that and more.

You have a unique opportunity here. As you read earlier, in this business, as in most businesses, you need to build a relationship before you build a business. This has created many new friends for me, and it can do the same for you. Some were friends before I got started and saw the same opportunity for themselves as I did. The rest are people who would never have been my friends had it not been for this business. Where could you work and have that happen?

The truth is you have a choice. You could ignore this opportunity and maintain your current lifestyle. With the tremendous growth that has been going on though, it's possible that some of your friends will get into it during the next few years. The question is, do you want to be the one to bring them in or would you prefer that someone else does? Either way, they'll probably still be your friends. But wouldn't it be great spending more time with them, while you all secure your future—*together?*

Here's a motto successful people use to motivate themselves to keep going: "I will do today as others will not, so I can live tomorrow as others cannot." Remember, *the difference between what you are today and what you want to be is what you do!* You're in the driver's seat.

Former Salesman and His Homemaker Wife—*Bubba and Sandy Pratt*

After an illustrious career as outside linebacker for the University of Florida, Bubba entered the business world intent on continuing his winning ways. He began his career as an automobile salesman, and the harsh realities of the working life became apparent.

Bubba remembers, "I had always been a person who didn't mind working hard to be successful. When I was a sophomore at Florida, *Sports Illustrated* magazine ran a feature article on the Gators. Coach Doug Dickey talked about me, saying that I had no respect for my body—that I would do whatever it took to get the job done. The problem in the sales world was that working hard didn't always mean financial rewards. Working hard, as I would soon learn, wasn't the same as working smart."

It took just four years for the Pratts to reach their goal of total financial freedom. Today, Bubba, Sandy, and their four children enjoy the fruits of their work and faith in this system. From homes to travel, Bubba's retirement from the auto dealership to debt free living—the rewards have been plentiful.

Emphasizes Sandy, "If you don't quit, you cannot fail in this business—no matter what happens."

Chapter 14
Where Do You Want to Be in 5 Years?
"The future belongs to those who believe in the beauty of their dreams."
Eleanor Roosevelt

Have You Been Planning Your Future?

What bills are due this week? What do you want to do this weekend? What do you want for your birthday? Where do you want to go on vacation?

These are questions you may ask yourself all the time. It's likely you ask them because you believe they're important. It's true you need to take care of your responsibilities and remember special people and occasions; but what about *you?* Are you getting lost in the shuffle? Who's asking the questions that will take care of you?

Recent studies indicate most people spend more time planning their annual vacation than their retirement. I believe some people may be procrastinating; but not everybody. Our society has painted a bleak picture of what retirement will probably be like with inflation and "Socialistic Insecurity." It's human nature to avoid thinking about what may be considered an unpleasant inevitable situation. Since, in most cases, no one has really shown us how to prepare properly, what's there to think about anyway?

You may be quite far from retirement age. But whether you are or not, let's take a look at your immediate future. What is your five-year plan? How will you assure that, in five years, you'll be where you want to be financially and otherwise? What dreams and goals do you plan to achieve between now and then? If you're like I was, you don't have any solid plans. Don't feel bad. Most people don't have plans. We have been conditioned since birth to study hard, finish school, get a good job, work 40 to 50 years, then retire. Not much more planning is needed in that scenario.

What Does Age Have to Do With Retirement?

Many people retire between 65 and 70 years of age. They may be asked to leave their jobs at that time; ready or not, they're gone. Many people are not financially ready to retire when the time comes. So, what happens? Some begin new careers at a fast food restaurant earning minimum wage to supplement their income. Imagine, after 40 to 50 years of hard work, they now need to work at a food service job. Wouldn't they rather be enjoying the benefits of retirement that they looked forward to for all those years?

Other people, some as young as 21, are already retired and never have to worry financially again. Did they inherit millions? Some people do, but not the ones we're discussing here. Others were able to retire according to traditional norms, but are enjoying every day of it because they are debt free and have a continuous, ongoing income. What do they know that you don't? Probably very little. They were just willing to dig their well before they were thirsty. They discovered that to get more out of life later, they had to do more now.

Have you ever complained about your income and having too much month left at the end of the money? If, on a weekly basis, you would invest in this business the time it takes you to read this book, it's possible you could equal or maybe even surpass your current income. And all the while you would still be working, and maintaining the security of your job or other business income.

Here's a solution for you to consider: Put some effort into building a *residual* income. Even though you may be able to work longer hours at your present job or business, or even get second job, your income basically stops when you stop working. Creating residual income is the key. The bottom line is *retirement doesn't take age; it takes money*. Money gives you options.

The Two-to-Five-Year Plan

Most of us will work for about 45 years before we can retire. If you average 2 weeks vacation per year, that means you'll have actually worked a little more than 43 years with a little less than 2 years off. If, however, you're willing to go for something more, you could, in 2 to 5 years, have the rest of your life to do what you *really* want to do! Isn't that an exciting thought?

If you worked a part-time job to supplement your income, how many hours could you work? Ten to twenty hours a week? How much would you earn? Around minimum wage, with no benefits? What would happen if you became ill and couldn't work? Would this extra income continue? Even if it did, how much are we talking about? If you worked 20 hours a week at $5.00 an hour, you'd earn $100 a week and, with 2 weeks for vacation, a total of $5,000 a year.

With some part-time effort in your business, over a period of time, you could be earning $3,000 to $5,000 a month in residual income. One of the great benefits of this system is that as you earn more money less effort is required to sustain it, as the residual income kicks in and multiplies. The more dedicated you are to following the system, the more success and time freedom you're likely to achieve. That just can't happen with a job or with most conventional businesses. It's the *duplication process* that makes it all possible. The more effort you put in now, while delaying gratification, the more you're likely to be rewarded later. Furthermore, when you build a solid organization, the rewards will last, unlike most paychecks that are here today and gone tomorrow. You can set up permanent income streams that will pay you and your heirs for generations to come.

Your efforts today are what can pay you down the road—handsomely. Start looking at your efforts as if they were investments designed to pay off big later. You wouldn't invest in the stock market each Monday and routinely sell all your stocks every Friday, would you? Of course not!

Many investors do what's known as dollar cost averaging. All that means is that you add a little each month to your portfolio regardless of whether the market is up or down. Historically, many people who have done this over a long period of time have come out way ahead.

What happens when you consistently invest your effort into your business? When you continue following the system each week even if you're not always seeing the results you want, and you do this over a sustained period of time, you may be very surprised at how large your investment grows. The real difference between this and the stock market is, you don't sell your investment (of following the system) to reap the greatest profit. *Your current success just **adds to** what you already have coming in from your past success!* When you have a solid, growing business, you don't need to do any more than you did the previous year, yet your income compounds, as duplication continues to multiply the effect of your previous efforts.

Plan Your Work—*Then Work Your Plan!*

Have you ever noticed that if you wait for the future to just happen, it's likely to catch you by surprise? Did you also observe that what happens is likely to be what *someone else* wants, not you? Yet, proper planning and gradual effort will allow you to have more control over your future, instead of it controlling you. Wouldn't you rather make the extra effort now, while you're able, rather than having to work later when you're older and it may be much more difficult? You begin small in the business—at zero, just like anyone else getting started. Then, as you grow, your efforts can compound into a distribution and income that can go on for a lifetime and beyond.

We all need a plan—a commitment—to take care of ourselves and our families. If we don't take charge of our own financial future, then we're leaving it up to someone else, like an employer. If somebody else holds the purse strings, they also decide our lifestyle. *I don't know about you, but I'm not putting in decades of effort only to have someone else tell me how to live.* I believe that life has much more to offer us than that. How about you?

I also believe that your reward is equal to your contribution. If you do more for others, you benefit yourself in the process. Then you can have more. This business is set up so that you're rewarded by getting what you want when you help enough other people get what they want.

Commit to doing something about your future. Do it today. Finish this book and ask the person who shared it with you to go into detail. Ask them any questions and clear up any reservations you may still have. Once you have all the facts, I believe you can then make an informed quality decision. It's totally up to you what you decide to do.

Chapter 15
Twelve Thought-Provoking Questions

"It's not whether you get knocked down,
it's whether you get up."
Vince Lombardi

It's Time for a Reality Check

When approached about an opportunity, some people get defensive and let us know they're doing okay. You can be glad if they're truly happy and satisfied with their station in life. Then again, maybe they're just scared and, being afraid to move forward, have convinced themselves that they're satisfied.

While it's true that they may regret it later, the fact is, you can't force anybody to do anything they don't want to do. Be aware that sometimes, when people are asked specific questions about their lives, reality can hit hard. They may not want to face or admit the truth.

At this point, it's important to ask yourself some key questions. Knowing where you stand will help you determine where you want to go. You want to go through life with as much focus and clarity as possible. Otherwise, you're like a ship without a rudder, unable to hold course, never getting where you want to go.

The following questions are just for you and your family. They're not part of an entrance exam and you aren't required to answer them to take advantage of this business. However, answering them could help you to make some decisions.

There are twelve in all. Skip them if you wish. Answer them if you dare!

How's Your Income?

My parents made more each year than the year before and were able to improve their lifestyle annually. However, things have changed. As *Fortune Magazine* said, "Most workers now barely keep pace with inflation." How about you?

My mom was home every day when I was growing up. However, when my wife and I had kids, they were in day care or with sitters for several years so that we could provide for them as well as my parents did. Keep in mind, my income level at the time was in the top 2 percent of the nation. I thought if our paychecks covered enough bills to get us to the next paycheck, we were doing okay. I wasn't prepared for the little things like children's medical expenses, bigger cars with higher insurance premiums, a larger home, and an adjustable rate mortgage that only knew one direction.

What about your wants? Do you have what you want or just what you think you need to have? For example, let's look at the difference between a new Corvette, an exciting sports car, and a '79 Pinto. Both of them have the potential to get you from point A to point B but if you had a choice which one would *you* pick? If you're working to your maximum potential, isn't it fair that you're able to have at least *one* thing you want? Absolutely! Say you have kids too. After you pay all your bills, put food on the table, pay for school clothes, and all the other standard household and child-rearing expenses, wouldn't it be nice to be able to do what you want with the rest?

Let's say you begin practicing delayed gratification and start saving for some things you want. You put a little of your pay aside each week so that, at some point, you can treat yourself to something special. Then suddenly, when you least expect it, the boss wants to see you and all the savings are suddenly spoken for. He tells you you're an excellent worker but the company has to downsize!

Do You Have Job Security?

Who can guarantee your employment? Your current employer? You? Were you aware that an average of over 3,000 people are laid off every day in the U.S. alone? The trend has shifted from only labor being let go to a point now where almost no one is safe.

Downsizing, rightsizing, or whatever you want to call it, is happening—even in profitable companies! In some cases, they size down to make their earnings sheet look even more attractive to the owners and shareholders.

Studies show that today's college grad is likely to have ten different jobs by the time they retire and as many as three complete career changes. That amounts to a new job every 4½ years. It's difficult to accumulate a pension under those conditions, so it's understandable why many people put off planning for their future or never do it at all! Making it week to week is often hard enough. That could be why most heart attacks occur on Monday mornings between 6 a.m. and 9 a.m., according to an article in *USA Today*.

I read another article in the *Manchester Union Leader* recently that said the best way to be secure in the workplace today is to begin getting in "workshape." That means developing a new *backup career* now to avoid the pitfalls of a surprise termination.

If you developed a solid secondary income that continued to grow each month, would you keep working at the same pace and place? For some of you the answer is yes because you enjoy your work. That's super. It's great that you have such a satisfying and rewarding career. But how much do you *really* like it? Would you do it for free?

Do You Have Time to Do What You Really Want to Do?

Are you able to spend as much time as you want with your family or doing the leisure activities you enjoy? Did you ever wait all year for your two-week vacation and then it rained most of the time? What did you end up doing? If you have children—what happens when your kids have a school play or a ballgame scheduled during your work hours? Do you need to scramble and beg for time off, or can you just take time off with no problem? If you woke up one morning and decided to just sleep in, would you need to quickly catch a virus and call in sick, or can you roll over (rather than roll out) with a clear conscience?

Most people who have time, have no money to enjoy it. The majority of us need to work to earn the money and when we finally have enough, there's often no time to do what we want to do. Many of us go from home to work, work to home, home to work, work to home, home to work, and so forth, in ad nauseam. And all most people get is two weeks off, if that. The kicker is, in many cases, *they* may even tell us which two weeks it has to be! And to top it off, a lot of people spend those two weeks painting the house or doing another big job they've been needing to get done. Yuk! It's not a real exciting scenario.

How Much Security Does Your Family Have?

Let's say you've got a great job. You're making good money, you come and go as you please, and you really enjoy your work. That's terrific. You're one of the fortunate few. However, if you become incapacitated or die, who would inherit your job and income? The answer is, of course, no one.

The truth is, in all likelihood, your lifestyle is dependent on your ability to show up for work and do what's expected of you. Pure and simple. If you don't go to work, you won't get paid.

Imagine a surgeon who earns a high six-figure income. What would happen if his hands became useless due to illness or injury? Aside from the medical bills, how would his family continue to enjoy their lifestyle? That is one of the reasons more professionals are attracted to this business, and its residual income aspect, every day.

You can talk about insurance and employee benefits all you want. The only person you can count on to secure your and your family's future is *you*. If you haven't taken the steps to provide for your family in the event of an emergency, it's likely someone else will control their lifestyle and destiny.

Is Job Satisfaction Enough for You?

How can you be satisfied at a job if you're worried about being laid off? It's difficult to give your best when you need to keep your eye out for the next job opportunity *just in case*.

With more middle management layoffs than ever before, the likelihood of moving up the corporate ladder is greatly reduced. Do you believe you have a great future at work? You may. Then again, you may not. You could be in the same place for a long time. But then again, economic conditions outside your control may mean you might be laid off a few years from now or even sooner.

Many people are like gerbils on a wheel. They run like crazy working up a sweat, but they never get anywhere.

You may be confident that you'll never be laid off. Hopefully, you never will. But, at the same time, there are lots of folks who've been surprised, to say the least, when *they* got the ax. You just never know. It pays to prepare yourself.

Does Your Education Guarantee Your Financial Future?

An associate of mine learned a tough lesson about the value of education in today's marketplace. He graduated from college and went on to earn his master's degree. After two more years of rigorous study, he got his Ph.D. He was now a full professor of mathematics at a prestigious university. Imagine his surprise when he found out that even with his substantial earnings, he couldn't afford tuition for his kids at the very school where he teaches!

My niece's first choice was an Ivy League school where the total cost for tuition, room and board, and other fees is $35,000 a year. My daughter is only 11. How much will it be when she's ready to go to college? If tuition is more than the average salary in the U.S., what happens to our kids? I know, there are student loans. Even so, a lot of kids won't even qualify because their parents' income is too high—yet not high enough to pay for college! Besides, even if they do qualify, what a great way to start your kids off in this world: inexperienced, competing for any job they can get, and deeply in debt.

What if You're Disabled?

According to the Society of Actuaries, if you're 35 years old, you are three times more likely to become disabled for three months or more than to die. Three months of little or no income. What would happen to your life?

Did you know that 65 percent of all bad credit is a result of disability? Even if they get some type of disability benefits, most people's expenses go up when they're disabled while their income drops significantly.

How About Your Retirement?

A report by Merrill Lynch states that today's baby boomers are saving only one third of what they need to save in order to retire. Something's got to give. They're the ones who may need to sell the home they've worked years to pay for and settle for a tiny place they can afford. Then they may justify it by saying the house was too big anyway. Maybe it was, but maybe it wasn't! The truth is, most people would prefer to live in a bigger house.

Here's another number. An article in an issue of *Fortune Magazine* reported this: "A couple in their late 30s earning a total of $85,000 a year will need $4.6 million to maintain their standard of living at 65." That's what such a couple would need to have invested to pay dividends equal to what they're now earning. With this business you have the opportunity to set up a residual income source that is like money in the bank. Think about it. Earning $50,000 a year in residual income is like getting 5 percent interest on $1,000,000!

Are You Happy With Where You're Living?

Do you live exactly where you want to live? Is your house the one you've always dreamed of? Or is it the one you settled for because the bank said you could afford it? (If your answer is the latter, you're not alone.) Do you own your home, or are you piling up rent receipts? (Most people who own their home are pretty well mortgaged to a financial institution who in reality owns their home.)

If you're wincing a little at these questions and ideas, you're not the only one. Most of us are so darn busy, we don't take the time to think about these things. And we all need to, that is if we're sick and tired of being sick and tired of the way things are and we're ready to do something about it. This system gives you a chance to do just that.

You deserve to have exactly what you want. You want your choices, like whether to buy a large or small home, to reflect what *you* really, really want and not just the economics of the situation. After all, it's *your life*, isn't it? Time's a marchin' on.

Is Personal Business Ownership for You?

Your best shot at success faces you every morning. When you look in the mirror you see your solution. That person is your ticket to financial freedom. As long as someone else signs your paycheck, they will determine where you can afford to live and what you can afford to drive. They tell you when you're to be at work and when you can play. Worst of all, every payday, they show you what *they* think you're worth. You're lucky if you're paid what *you* think you're worth. Are you?

To get paid what you're worth, consider following advice from J. Paul Getty: Number one of his "Six Guidelines for Financial Success" is "You must be in business for yourself."

Are You Willing to *Do* Something?

You have a general idea of what you need to do to improve your financial picture through the power of duplication. In order to change your answers to the questions in this chapter from what they are to what you want them to be, are you willing to put in an extra 8 to 15 hours a week for the next 2 to 5 years?

In five years, you will be five years older. Will you be where you want to be or still in the same position? Will you be kicking yourself for not doing something to change your situation? Or will you be happy that you took action? Will you continue putting off the inevitable until things get worse? Or will you say, "Enough is enough. I've had it. I'm movin' on"?

Either way, you've made a decision. If you remain as you are, which is perfectly legal, it's your decision. You can blame the economy, the market, the boss, or the other guy, but it's you and you alone who gets the credit. However, if you do decide to do something about it, and take action, I believe you will feel a tremendous weight lifted from your shoulders. If you've been procrastinating, you'll feel a great sense of relief as soon as you simply make the decision to do something. As someone once said, "Deciding is half the battle."

How About Happiness?

With all this talk about money and success, what about being happy? Isn't that what everyone wants? Recently, an investigative TV news team interviewed people all across the U.S. to determine what it took for people to be happy. They discovered three prime ingredients. The happiest people had: 1) Strong faith; 2) A purpose for their lives; and 3) Control over what they did in life.

Just think about it for a minute. What makes you happy? Those three things? If not them, then what? Do you have what makes you happy in your present situation? If not, would you like to?

I suggest you get back to the person who shared this book with you and ask for more details. Ask to meet some more people who are successful *and* happy. Discover how you can be that way too.

Chapter 16
Your Next Move
"It's choice—not chance—
that determines your destiny."
Jean Nidetch

Now What?

There are a couple directions you can take from here. You could, of course, reject the entire concept and settle back into what you're doing. Or you could make a list of your questions about this system and how it could help you reach your goals. Then you could ask the person who shared this book with you to go into more detail, or introduce you to somebody who can.

This presents you with an opportunity to make an important decision that will affect your future in one way or another. And remember, not deciding is a decision too and all decisions have consequences.

No matter what you may decide to do however, you owe it to yourself to at least finish reading this book. This way you'll have a better picture of this opportunity and the possibilities it may hold for you and your family.

Facts and Figures

If the dream is big enough, the facts don't count. That statement has become a motto for many of those who are serious about this business. If you're not quite ready to dream as big as you can, or have a big dream and still want more information, hang on. There are plenty of documents showing industry trends, the full financial strength of this business, and a complete bonus schedule—all of which are available to you for the asking.

If you like numbers, I can tell you that hundreds of millionaires have developed as a result of this system during the last 25 years. This business can't guarantee wealth; no business can. However, when you follow this system, you'll get an education found nowhere else and, you'll be associated with some of the finest people you'll ever know. You're likely to get more recognition for each accomplishment, big or little, than most people get during their entire lifetime. This, coupled with the financial success you can achieve through this business, is a combination that's hard to beat. If there's anything better out there, please tell me. I'd sure like to know. I always keep an open mind.

Go to a Seminar and Check It Out

Sometime within the next few weeks, there's likely to be a seminar near you—it could be your deciding factor. Each seminar is broken into two sessions. The first half is a teaching session. This is where one or two of the more successful associates shares what they did to achieve their success. You could find the missing ingredient in what they share that will help you decide what you want to do.

The second session is my personal favorite. This is where the people who taught earlier, tell their story. They openly discuss the sometimes seemingly impossible challenges they had to overcome along the line to get where they are. Perhaps they went through what you're going through right now, or something similar. In any case, you'll see a bigger picture of this business and perhaps learn how it may be just what you're looking for.

These people will share *why* they got into the business and some of the funny things that happened as they were striving to become successful. And these associates come from all walks of life. I've heard speakers who *were* doctors, lawyers, and other professionals when they got into the business, but have since moved on. And then there was a mechanic with a third-grade education. The things these people had in common, though, was their dream for a better life and the determination to make it happen.

Many of them were unsure at first, as you may be. Some had to be shown this business several times. It's important that you see it presented as many times as it takes for you to be sure of your decision. Also, if you'd like, you can ask about the possibility of attending more than one seminar so you can meet more people and learn more about the business. It's a good idea to be a searching doubter. No matter what you'd like to accomplish, seek the truth and you will find it.

Will It Work and Can You Do It?

The industry was originally conceived in the late 1940s and, as I mentioned before, is now being taught by business-people worldwide. It's enabling many folks from ordinary backgrounds to become financially independent and live the life they want.

The involvement of hundreds of doctors, lawyers, accountants, and other professionals shows its credibility. And interestingly enough, nobody I know of who's successful in this business wants to go back to the often-grueling schedules of the professions they once loved! The time freedom is their hot button.

Hundreds of Fortune 500 companies have chosen our system as a great way to move their goods and services. We can also do business in over 80 countries. Industry-wide, revenues are over $50 billion and our particular system has expanded as much as 20 percent a year.

The real question is not whether it works, but will it work for you? Do you really want a better life? How serious are you about achieving your goals and dreams? Do you have a strong desire to do so? If so, that's a great start. In fact it's key to your success. Lots of people have done it, and you can too!

This is not a business that requires you to have special skills or a certain level of education. This business was founded on the principles of Free Enterprise. Those, like our corporate supplier, who provide a better level of service with superior products will find long-lasting success in the marketplace.

This system and this business works 100 percent of the time for 100 percent of the people who work it. It will always work for those who commit to their own success 100 percent. You've probably already discovered this about yourself. You'll do whatever you make up your mind to do, when you want the anticipated results badly enough. You do whatever it takes to make it happen.

Remember, in the final analysis where you are and where you're going in life is always *your* decision. You may say, "My wife (husband) and my boss make the decisions." All this means is that you've decided to delegate your decision-making power to them for whatever reason. The fact is that no one forces anyone to succeed or fail, except themselves. The results you get in life are totally up to you.

Do you feel you're not getting where you want to go, doing what you're doing? If so, what's holding you back besides you? When you encounter an obstacle, ask yourself, "How can I work this out?" Be a possibility thinker. Look for solutions and focus on the benefits of achieving your dreams.

Questions are what we ask when we're shaping our destiny. Instead of asking yourself, "What have I got to lose?" turn the question around and ask, "What have I got to WIN?"

It's Totally Up to You

You can't be sold this opportunity or anything else for that matter and expect to be successful. Besides which, nobody likes to be sold. People do like to buy, though. However, people only buy when there's something in it for them. Unlike many things, this business isn't for sale. It's just here for those who want to move on and take advantage of the power of duplication.

All anyone can do is present the facts, provide a little insight about how it works, answer your questions, and leave the rest to you. If you see something, great. If not, that's fine too.

If you say no, is that no for now or no forever? If you haven't already done so, ask yourself these two questions: *"If not this, what?"* and *"If not now, when?"* If you decide that no is your answer, you can change your mind later. But how long do you want to wait to achieve your goals and dreams? In my own case, some of the people I shared it with didn't get started until a year or two went by. Now they're moving ahead. The only regret they have is that they didn't get started sooner. They're sorry they procrastinated. There's no *perfect* time to get started in the sense that there's unlikely to be a time when there's nothing standing in the way. There will always be stuff you need to work around to be successful.

The Power Noes

Where else can you get into such a huge business virtually risk free and where everything available to assist your growth is optional? Many folks get in just to buy products to save some time and money. They like the convenience of ordering out of a catalog by phone or over the Internet—with delivery to their door! Others get into it because they believe it's the best and maybe the only chance they will ever have to be successful. Whatever *your* reason would be and however big your business gets, the rules to get started remain the same:

◆ No inventory required.
◆ No buildings to rent or buy.

- ◆ No payroll necessary.
- ◆ No employees and the hassles of having them.
- ◆ No minimum orders.
- ◆ No quotas.
- ◆ Even your start-up kit is 100 percent satisfaction guaranteed or your money back!

This is a business that won't put you in debt. There are no loans to get and be approved for. The business is yours; you have no boss to tell you what to do. You make the decisions. The support system offers the guidance that could help you avoid some common mistakes. Yet, since it's your own independent business, you're free to accept or reject the direction that's offered.

Since you've taken enough time to read this far, you probably have enough time to make a difference in your life and the lives of those around you. Granted, it could require some juggling of your current responsibilities. But you can do it if you really want to.

Things are changing. In fact, life is change. Have you noticed that few things stay the same for very long? For example, look at a recent credit card bill. (If you don't have one, look in a general mail-order catalog.) Some of the things on the bill or in the catalog weren't even available a few short years ago. But by the time some people pay some of these things off, they're no longer any good and may need to be replaced. *Change is inevitable; growth is optional.* Why not move on your options? What are you waiting for?

Chapter 17
Dare to Dream!

*"If one advances confidently in the direction
of his dreams, and endeavors to live the life which
he has imagined, he will meet with success
unexpected in common hours."*
Henry David Thoreau

Everything Good Starts With a Dream

Did you ever want something so much you could taste it? Whatever it was, you absolutely *had* to have it. If you had to skip a few lunches during the week or even stay out of restaurants for a month to save the money to get it, that wasn't a problem. The sacrificing was the easy part. You knew it was worth doing whatever it took because you decided you couldn't live without it.

That's the power of a dream. When you *have to have* something badly enough, don't you always seem to find a way to get it? If you told me today you had no money and your car broke down on the way home, wouldn't you somehow come up with a way to fix it? Well, if your financial vehicle isn't running the way you want, doesn't it make sense to do what it takes to get it fixed?

Many people think it's corny to keep talking about dreams. But if you don't dare to dream, you'll just get the status quo—same old, same old. You may be somewhat safe, but you may be sorry, too.

If you don't take action, nothing will change unless someone else makes the change (layoff, involuntary job transfer, and the like) for you. *If you keep doing what you've been doing, you'll continue to get what you've been getting, or maybe worse.* So start to dream for all you've ever hoped for. When you focus on these things, you will be on your way to having them. *You get what you focus on.*

The Difference Between Have To and Want To

If you just *want* to get a new car, if you just *want* to go on vacation, or if you just *want* a nicer place to live, you'll probably never have them. The statement, "It would be nice if...." just isn't strong enough to propel you to do what it takes to make it happen. You are just making a *wish*. If all you're doing is just wishing for something or even casually commenting that you need something, it's likely you'll quit working for it as soon as it becomes inconvenient or the least bit difficult. There are lots of needy people out there and most everybody wants for something.

Needs and wants just don't cut it. They're weak and as a result, it's likely you'll begin to justify not going for it. You may tell yourself, "It's too materialistic." Or you may *make excuses.* The bottom line is, you won't get out of life what you want. You'll be at the mercy of other people who'll dictate your lifestyle as they follow *their* dream.

Dreaming turns want to into have to. It turns maybes into priorities. It lights the fire of passion inside you and makes you fight for what you really, really want. You may build this business for a new car, new house, or a nice vacation. Yet, when you also dream of having more time with your family, long-term security for them, and the removal of all financial pressure, you can have those material things as a by-product.

Focusing on whatever you've decided you can't live without is what's important. When it becomes a dream, a passion, a have to, you will do whatever it takes to get where you want to go. *All truly successful people have at least one big dream that drives them.* And the more dreams they have, the better. This is one of the major keys to success.

Write It Down

When I was selling cars, one of the things every customer wanted was to have all my promises put in writing, and understandably so. That way there was no backing out of the deal I was offering them. This same rule holds true when you buy real estate. If it isn't written down, you may not get it (depending on the integrity of the seller or agent).

However, when I ask people if they've written down their dreams and goals, they usually look at me as though I've got two heads! Why would you expect a stranger to make commitments to you in writing and not expect the same of yourself?

The expression "Out of sight, out of mind" is very true. If we don't see things often enough, we're likely to forget about them. It's human nature. But when you write your goals and dreams down, you're taking the first step to committing to them. It's powerful. Your brain has to process them in order for you to write them down! Mentally, you begin to hold yourself to them.

The key is to place what you've written where you'll see it often. Some people put it up in one or more places, like on their bathroom mirror, on the wall beside their bed, on their refrigerator, on the dash of their car, or in their office or work area.

You also need to review them daily and adjust for changes as you move along. (You may need to rewrite it as you get a clearer picture of what you have in mind.) It's okay to change your dreams and goals as you grow. This way they keep up with you and the different needs you'll have as success becomes a reality. Get excited about them and work toward attaining them.

Tell This to the Person Who Shared This Book With You

Pressure. Most people don't like it. Yet, if you understand a little physics, you can use it to your advantage. Why do you think a volcano erupts? As you may know, the pressure builds up from inside until it can't be contained any longer. Then in what direction does it erupt? Straight up! If you want to move on up, it's important that you find some pressure.

No one likes to fail. This is often why some of us don't write things down. We may be afraid of failing. Often what we're really afraid of is rejection. In reality though, that rejection could teach you what you need to know to build up just the right amount of pressure to shoot you straight to the top. What you may want to do is share your dreams with the family member, friend, or acquaintance who has shared this book with you. Tell them what you want to accomplish for yourself and your family. Ask them if they can help you or know someone who can. You're not necessarily ready to do anything yet—you're just looking at the possibilities. You're sorting it out to see what you might want to do.

They can also help you to stay on track. Whenever the friends who shared this business with me and I are together, they always ask me how I'm doing. They're sincerely interested in me and my success. As I've said earlier, all of your friends may not join you. But that doesn't matter. After all, in most cases, you have different jobs, don't you? When you tell the person who shared this book with you about your dreams, it may inspire you to work a little harder toward making them come true. Even if you became successful just to prove you could (both to yourself and others), would that make your success any less worthwhile?

Drive It, Tour It, and Put Up Pictures

If you're dreaming of buying a new car, what have you done to make it more real, to make your dream come alive for yourself? You may want to go over to your local car dealership, find the car you want, and have them set you up on a test drive. Smell the interior, listen to the engine, feel the ride, and see it in your driveway. Have someone take a picture of you sitting in the car. Take home a brochure; be sure they give you the interior and exterior color chips. Cut out the picture you like the most and put it on your refrigerator or someplace else where you'll see it several times a day. Write the date next to it that you'd like to pick one up.

If it's a home you're looking for, attend an open house. Have the agent show you around. Size up each room and picture it fully furnished exactly the way you'd like it. Remember the sound and smell in each room. The echo of emptiness is a powerful sound. It leaves space for you to imagine you're hearing your family and friends making noise in the house. If it's the exact house you've pictured in your dream or you like certain features, bring a camera. Take pictures of each room so you can envision how you would decorate them once you sign the papers. Put the date you'd like to own it on your refrigerator. You may need to reset it, but at least you have a target to shoot for.

Dreams are where it all begins. Without them, life is empty and this or any other opportunity is just another job. And you're probably not looking for just another job, are you?

Dreams change work into opportunity. They're the birthplace of wealth of all kinds—not just financial wealth. For example, interpersonal relationships can grow stronger when you're going towards a common goal or dream.

If you have children, you know firsthand that they learn by example. You can show them by your actions that they too can be, do, and have anything they want when they have a dream and do what it takes to make it happen. This is the surest way to be a hero. That's part of what this business is all about. We're also paving the way for our children to follow their dreams and fulfill their potential.

If you're still unsure, the only thing holding you back from taking action is *you*. Your life is made up of a series of choices. Should you choose to get started, you will be rewarded as you grow and create distribution. You can also choose to remain where you are. In either case, you've made a conscious decision for your future.

When this opportunity was first shared with me, I was a searching doubter, just as you may be. That's healthy. So, I checked it out by meeting people who were already successful in this business. I asked them plenty of questions and got the answers I needed to make my decision. No matter what field you might look into, it just makes good sense to talk to people who are successful at it.

After all my doubts were laid to rest, I got started. I had a dream of spending more time with my family. As a husband and a father, I wanted to set up a financial situation where my family would be taken care of—just in case I couldn't produce or was taken out of the picture. Now I don't worry about that anymore, and it feels great!

Chapter 18
What if This Thing Really Works?

*"All of your dreams can come true,
if you have the courage to pursue them."*
Walt Disney

Facts Are Facts

There's enough public documentation to prove, beyond a shadow of a doubt, that this business works. On a personal level, I've met many people whose lives have changed as a result of this business. I know a young couple who started their business at age 19 and are retired from their jobs and financially independent at age 26. I also met a couple recently who are in their 70s who are earning more now than when they were employed.

Is it a guaranteed success package? Absolutely not. Yet, when you follow the success system and duplicate those who went before you who are where you want to be, your life will change for the better. When you get started, but then go home and do nothing, you won't need an accountant to figure out how much you're earning. Like any endeavor, your success is largely determined by how much effort you put into it using the principles you've been taught.

When any of us start something new, we need to be open-minded and teachable. We need to listen to the experts. Fortunately, with this business, unlike conventional businesses or franchises, you have no real financial risk but a great opportunity to grow.

Sometimes the fact that you have no investment in inventory or employees may make this seem like a little something you do on the side. If you have that attitude, you'll ultimately prove yourself correct. To build a big business, you need to treat it like a big business. When you understand the power of this business system, you'll know that you can achieve whatever level of success and security you're serious about achieving. Other people have and you can too. The key is to think big. As Dr. David Schwartz says in his book *The Magic of Thinking Big,* "See what can be, not just what is." Anyone who really wants to move on could benefit from reading that book.

Even though this business is simple, it isn't a free ride. Like anything worthwhile, it takes effort. Whenever you start a business, you need to practice delayed gratification. When you first start a conventional business, much of your money goes right back into it. In this business however, you're basically investing your time. You simply don't need a lot of money to start this business.

As your business grows, you not only improve your financial picture, you also gain time freedom, which gives you more options. The time you choose to invest doing the business depends on your business and personal goals as well as the lifestyle you desire. You can do more or less. You can choose to spend more time on other activities you enjoy. This is exactly the opposite of most conventional businesses. In fact, most traditional small business owners are actually owned by their own business; it consumes their life and they'll readily admit it. Sure they may only work half the time; they just need to decide which 12 hours it's going to be!

You may still be asking, "Will this system work for me?" And there's only one person who can accurately answer that. When you look in the mirror ask that person, "What is your dream? Are you willing to do what it takes to make it come true?" When you are, this system can work for you as long as you follow the pattern for success that's already been established. Remember, you have nothing to lose and everything to gain when you do whatever it takes to achieve your dream.

Why Isn't Everyone Doing It?

I could give you some long drawn out answers discussing the psychology of why some people succeed while others don't. I could tell you that this business isn't for everyone. I could also tell you there are certain people who may not even qualify. The bottom line is, there's no simple answer. It all depends. Nevertheless, the fact is we all make choices in life and we all get to live with them.

Some critics have told me this business too simple to be any good. What I'd like to know is, who made up the rule that good things and good opportunities have to be complicated?

It's becoming more and more evident that most of us would like our lives to be simpler. As a result, millions have been made by inventors finding simpler ways for us to enjoy life. Why shouldn't this be the case for business? Why can't a business be successful and simple at the same time? The answer is it can and, in this case, it is. Some may say this is too good to be true. But I think you'll find that those folks haven't given themselves the chance to be successful in this business.

This is the business of the 21st Century. More people are using this system every day. Paul Zane Pilzer, the famous economist, author, and presidential advisor, has stated that *the next wave of wealth will come from the distribution of products rather than manufacturing them.* He also said that the business we are discussing is already on the cutting edge and is ready for tremendous growth during the 21st Century.

Does this business work? Does anything work? *People work.* This is just an opportunity. Taking action is key to making anything work!

Some of you may still be asking yourself, "What have I got to lose?" As suggested before, you may, instead, consider asking yourself, "What have I got to WIN?" This is an opportunity for you to achieve your dreams. It's totally up to you what you do with it. How serious are you about what you say you want? Are you serious enough to do something about it? Just be honest with yourself and make the best decision for you and your family.

Chapter 19

Are You Saying, "I'm Interested— Now What"?

"I do not fear failure. I only fear the slowing up of the engine inside me which is pounding, saying, 'Keep going, someone must be on top, why not you?'"
George S. Patton, Jr.

What Do I Do Next?

There is no way you can learn everything about this business from this book. Besides, someone probably already gave you an idea of how it works. The purpose of this book is to let you know that there's a vehicle you can use to set yourself up to live your dream. It won't happen overnight; nothing worthwhile does. But I believe you'll find whatever time you invest will be worth it.

It's likely you read this book out of curiosity; you wanted to learn more. If you've been reading it with an open mind, you've probably had one of two things happen.

Number one, you're now more curious than ever about how you could do this thing. It seems like a great opportunity but you need some questions answered. Go to the person who shared this book with you. Ask your questions and insist that they spell the whole plan out in detail. If they're new too, they can find someone with more success under their belt who can give you the information you need.

It can get pretty exciting realizing you can achieve your dreams without quitting your job or selling your current business, moving away, or borrowing money. Ask that person to give you all the details of the potential and how it has affected people in your area. Also, remember that it's likely they know of a seminar where you can meet some of these people and learn more.

Get ready to go. Strike while the iron's hot. The person who shared this book with you has access to all the information and support you'll need to get going. Listen to them. The trail has already been blazed. Follow in their footsteps, and you stand a much better chance of succeeding. Trust their advice. Your success is their success. The more they're able to help you, the better for you and the better for them! It's a win-win situation!

Nothing's for Everyone

The other possibility is, after evaluating what you've seen so far, you've decided this isn't for you—at least not now. No problem; nothing's for everyone! The point is, you're in the driver's seat. After receiving and considering some information, the decision is yours.

Consider this: At the rate this business is growing, some of your friends are likely to get in or maybe they're already in! These people may be current friends or ones you haven't met yet, but some will do this. If you don't get in and share in the rewards of their success, someone else will. Even if you don't want to do this but you find a few friends who do, you could still enjoy some of the rewards. Either way, it's your decision.

I shared this business with a friend and he said it wasn't for him and it wouldn't work. I saw him a year later and he asked me how it was going. I told him, "We did $6.3 billion last year without you and this year we'll do $7.5 billion." He interrupted and said, "Not without me, you won't." He's now building a successful business.

It's okay if you're still not sure whether this business is for you. You may just need more details. The person who shared this book with you is considerate; they'll be patient with you as you sort out what's best for you and your family. You want to be careful, though, that you aren't suffering from "paralysis of analysis." Some people believe they have to know everything to get started.

The truth is that this is pretty much a learn as you go business. That's part of the fun of it. You go at your own speed and get a handle on what to do as you move along. The key is to focus on your dream so you can blast through any obstacles that come your way. Others have, and you can too.

No matter what you may choose to do to improve your life, I wish you all the best. But *do something*. The government isn't going to make things better for you and your family. It's all up to you. As the saying goes, "If it is to be, it's up to me!"

From Wall Street to Main Street

The *Wall Street Journal* calls us a "sleeping giant." They've reported the fact that we're growing at a rate of 20 percent a year and have been for a few decades. From a financial stability point of view, our corporate supplier is debt free and has millions of dollars of capital at its disposal. We're taking full advantage of the growing interactive age.

There are homes already built with bar code scanners to read and order products. In the near future, they will be drop shipped to your home within 24 to 48 hours. We have the distribution channels already in place.

I've saved this for last because some people would see how big this business already is and may be surprised by its size. But just keep this in mind—it's only grown over the years because of people like you and me who have a vision. They can picture how their life could be improved and what it would be like living their dream.

Just a Suggestion

If you're willing to invest a few minutes, over a cup of coffee or a soda with the person who shared this book with you, perhaps they can cover some things I missed. Since they know you and hopefully what your dreams and goals are, they're in a better position to meet your needs. You owe it to yourself to get all the information you need to make a quality decision for you and your family.

Whatever you decide, be sure to thank the person who was kind enough to share this book with you. They paid you a compliment, and may have done you a favor, by sharing this opportunity with you. There are millions of people who have *never* been approached and are unaware of the potential of this business. As mentioned earlier, one of the advantages of this business is you can choose who you would like to have associate with you. Doesn't it feel good to know someone thought enough of you and what you stand for to make you *their* choice?

Epilogue

"Life is the sum of all your choices."
Albert Camus

Check It Out, Check It Out, Check It Out!

At the beginning of the book I told you a bit about my background and some of the reasons I chose to take this direction with my life. Your growth in this business, as is anyone else's, is in direct proportion to how much of it is in your heart versus how much is in your head. Your head sees what's in it for you and how to do it. That's the mechanics. Anyone can master that.

Your heart, on the other hand, widens your vision to see what's in it for those you care about and most importantly, WHY you could do this. I have discovered that once you know WHY you want something, the how takes care of itself. When you put your efforts into helping others succeed, your success can be greater than you may have ever imagined.

Congratulate yourself for reading this far. Many people complain about how they are unhappy about their current situation. But unfortunately, that's all they do—complain. You have set yourself apart. You are a doer—*a dreamer*. You may not realize it or believe it yet. But you have what it takes to learn what you need to know about this business, determine what's best for you and your family, and make a quality decision.

You may hear all kinds of comments from those who want to protect you from the harm that comes from *rocking the boat*. Things like, "Talk to so and so. He tried that and it didn't work." Ask yourself: If you were ill would you take advice from someone who *tried* medical school or would you prefer talking to a practicing doctor with a medical degree?

Talk to people who are succeeding in this business, and then decide if it's for you. *Check it out, check it out, check it out!* Your and your family's future is at stake and you owe it to yourself and to them to learn as much as you can and do something about it. The ball is in your court.

Your Life Is in Your Hands

To close, I'll leave you with a little story…

High on a hilltop, overlooking a beautiful village lived a wise old man. Children from the area were taught to seek his guidance and respect his teachings.

One day, two boys came up with a plan to confuse the old man. They caught a tiny bird and headed for the top of the hill. Before they got to the man's house, one of the boys cupped the little bird in his hands. They knocked on the door and were invited in—the old man loved children.

"Wise old man," the boy with the bird said, "Can you tell me if the bird I have in my hands is dead or alive?"

The old man gazed silently at the boys and said, "If I tell you the bird you have locked in your hands is alive, you will close your hands and crush the life out of it. If I tell you the bird is dead, you will open your hands and it will fly away to freedom.

"Son, in your hand you hold the power of life and death, bondage and freedom. You have the power to choose destruction and the end of a spirit and a song. Or you can choose to set the bird free so it has a future with all its potential. You are wise to know you can choose between life and death.

"If you allow my answer to determine whether the bird lives or dies, you will have given away your power. You will have also given away your responsibility to make the correct choice, and to rejoice in your own strength, wisdom, and potential."

The boys came down the hill a bit wiser. The old man, in respecting their desire to test themselves and his authority, proved to be a leader and a teacher. By refusing to cooperate with them, he contributed to their self-awareness and personal development.

You are now in a position to make a decision for yourself and your family. You have the power to choose, and it's your accumulated choices, made one at a time, that largely determine the life you lead. You can blindly follow the opinions and hearsay of others or seek the truth and make up your own mind.

Just the fact that you have read this book up to this point indicates you are doing your best to make wise choices. You are exploring the possibilities of rising above your circumstances and going forward to live your dreams. I applaud you for that. This could be a turning point in your life. It's all up to YOU!

If you'd like to know how to get started, keep reading...

Appendix

How to Get Started

*"The secret of success in life is
for a man to be ready for his
opportunity when it comes."*
Benjamin Disraeli

How Much Money Is Enough?

I know many people in other occupations and businesses who earn hundreds of thousands of dollars. Yet, if they quit tomorrow, their income would be lost and difficult to replace. If they're in debt, like most of them are, they could be in serious financial trouble. However, if they were debt free, they would need a lot less income.

As we discussed earlier, let's say you're like most homeowners and have a 30-year mortgage. What would happen when you build an income that allows you to make two mortgage payments each month instead of just one? When I first saw this opportunity, the person sharing it asked me that very question. I told them it would take 15 years, but as you may recall, I was wrong.

When you double your payments on a 30-year mortgage so the second payment is applied directly to the principal, you would own your house free and clear in only 6½ years! (Banks generally don't want you to know this. They'd like to stay on *your* payroll and keep getting your interest payments, which are you hard-earned *after-tax* dollars!)

When I heard that, I got angry with the bank, but I also got excited. Understand, I still had my job. That meant, in 6½ years, I would be able to save the money I had been using to

131

pay my mortgage. It also meant that the increasing extra income from my business could go into savings and investments too.

It's amazing how fast your money grows when you stop making the bank rich by wasting *your money* on interest. Ask yourself this: "How would I feel knowing our house is totally ours, free and clear, and my family *never* again has to worry about the bank ever foreclosing on us?"

Now you may be asking, "How can I do it? Where do I start? What do I do?" These were the exact same questions racing through my mind when I saw this opportunity.

Begin With the End in Mind

Stephen R. Covey, bestselling author of *The 7 Habits of Highly Effective People* tells us to "Begin with the end in mind." In other words, how much would you need to earn, outside your job income, to quit your job? For most people, earning $40,000 to $100,000 a year in *additional* income, plus sufficient savings, would be enough for them to retire comfortably from their job. What's even more exciting is that, unlike most jobs, your income from this business can not only sustain, but it can also grow, even *without* your daily effort.

As a matter of fact, the bigger and more solidly you build your business, the less effort is required of you personally to make it work—thanks to the benefits of the duplication process. Try making that happen when you get into a more conventional business, loaded with overhead. To increase your income, you'd have to put in more time, and most likely, hire employees. (Would hiring employees be worth the expense and difficulties you'd encounter? Having employees may actually *reduce* your bottom line!) On the other hand, using *duplication* allows you to *leverage* your time and, therefore, *multiply* your effectiveness. As Archimedes once said, "Give me a lever long enough, and I can move the earth." Yes, leverage *is* the key.

If you shared with someone that they could generate $3,000 a month *extra* and you weren't earning that yourself, would they believe you? How would they know this business works and what could cause them to build it with you?

You would simply show them people who were in their same or a similar career or situation and are now successful. You would have an opportunity to introduce them to such people at a meeting like you may have just attended. Or you could ask to attend a seminar where, as we discussed, they would do business training and share their personal story and experiences in building their business. And perhaps you may even get to meet with them, talk with them directly, and learn even more.

Did McDonald's begin franchising the first day of operation? Of course not. They worked out all the bugs they could with the first few restaurants. They designed the system so finely that few people question the McDonald's opportunity anymore. That's similar to this business. This system's been developed and fine-tuned to the point where anyone who is serious can duplicate it to build the success they want.

Now let's suppose that over the next 12 to 18 months you build this business and create a solid secondary income. Once you grow to this point, some or most of your income is likely to be residual and could continue without your additional effort. If you're unable to work or are taken out of the picture, the residual income continues coming in to support your family for the life of your business. That could give you a degree of security you may not now have. Would your current job or business give you that kind of benefit?

Can you imagine the feeling of freedom knowing this income is virtually automatic when you build this business to a certain level? Doesn't that benefit alone make it worth considering?

Self-Use Is Simply Being Loyal to Your Own Business

If you owned a gas station, where would you fill up? What if your competition's gas was a few cents a gallon cheaper? Wouldn't you still fill up at your own pumps?

From the first day you come on board it's important to create the mindset that this is *your* business. And what's the best way to get other people to do business with you? *First, do business with yourself!* Shop from the convenience of your own home for products and services available from your own business.

If you had a Cadillac dealership, for example, you wouldn't drive a Lincoln from a dealership down the road, would you? You'd drive a Caddy that you bought from yourself. Your friends and associates would know you believe in Cadillacs because you drive one! That's the best example you can set. When they want to buy a Caddy, they'd come to you, right?

When I first got into this business, I was earning a good living. We had nearly everything we wanted, yet we lacked the time to enjoy it. I got excited when I discovered I could buy the same products from myself that I used to buy at malls and supermarkets. And they would be shipped right to my home—at independent business owner discounts, no less!

Considering the time we used to spend at the stores and the malls, we saved a *lot* of time. We could use that time to do something together, as a family, besides shop. Then, of course, there's the money savings realized by *not* having to go to the store—gas, maintenance, and the like.

Here's the key concept of this business: *By saving time and money by buying from yourself; by sharing your products and services with a few people—some of whom may choose to buy at a discount or become your retail clients; and by sharing these ideas with others, you can create the level of success and wealth you need to live your dream.*

How Does the Self-Use System Work?

Remember, you're not required to buy anything. It's a choice. There are no minimums, no quotas, and no limited territories. You can share it with whomever you want, any time you choose to, almost anywhere in the world.

You simply *buy from yourself* the things you normally use or would like to use. As you find the quality of the products equals or exceeds what you'd been buying from stores (that didn't pay you to shop there), you begin to tell others about your results. Some may choose to join you; others may simply want to save time and money and buy at a discount or just save time and be retail clients.

Most People Don't Like to Sell or Be Sold, but Everyone Likes to Buy!

As you've probably gathered by now, you're not going door to door trying to sell anyone anything. That generally doesn't work because most people don't want to do it and a lot of people aren't home! They simply buy from catalogs or on the Internet and you make money. They save time and you make the difference between your cost as an independent business owner and the retail price. Frankly, I can't understand why anyone would want to buy at retail, but some folks still do.

Consider those who shop at malls and other retail stores. You're probably still doing it yourself! If so, how come? The answer is quite simple. We're all creatures of habit. But we're also adaptable to beneficial change. The question is: "Will you change your buying habits to save time and money on things you're already buying?"

Most businesspeople speak in terms of volume, and so do we. Your volume is used to establish the rate at which you earn income. The person who shared this book with you can see to it that you get a more detailed explanation, if you'd like. If fact, they may have given you information with this book that will tell you more.

You buy products at independent business owner discounts, some of your family members, friends, and acquaintances buy from catalogs or the Internet, and you make extra income. You're probably not ready to retire yet, but hang in there; you just got started.

The great thing is, you're not in debt like someone who started a conventional or franchise business is likely to be. Those businesses often look good on the surface, but the new owner probably owes the bank, or someone, a *lot* of money! They have a lot of work to do—*just to get to zero*. With this business you don't have to dig yourself out of the hole before you start making money.

Now, consider what it's really worth: You still have the security of your current job or business; you're spending your money on what you would normally buy *anyway;* and you're even pocketing some profit! What would happen if you apply that extra money to your credit cards? You could pay them off more quickly and reduce or eliminate the finance charges. Wouldn't that be great? You could then put your former monthly payments into your savings account instead of making the credit card company richer.

And this is only the beginning. By merely changing old habits, you begin saving time and money. You simply started *buying from yourself* from the comfort of your own home and sharing this idea and the products and services with others. You not only saved the time of running from one store to the next, like you used to, but you also saved the money you had been contributing to the stores' profits. *You've shifted your loyalty from the stores to your own family business!*

You may be saying to yourself, "But I don't like to sell," or "I can't sell." Most people getting into this business feel that way. Then they found that sharing was all they really needed to do. As they listened to other people talk throughout the day, they'd pick up on some needs they could fill with the products or services available through this business. They've made some money and you can too. While most people don't want to sell, many enjoy *sharing*. They use the products and services themselves, and find it easy to *share* them.

Did you ever share seeing a great movie or reading a good book with someone and then they went and did that? Well, they duplicated you. But you didn't get paid for it. In this business however, when you share it with someone and, as a result, products and services get purchased, you make money! *Remember, most people don't like to sell or be sold. But everybody likes to buy!*

If one of your neighbors or someone else comments on the products you have around the house, mentions something they need to buy, or wonders where your extra time and money are coming from, they may be interested in learning about this business. If you haven't already done so, then you'll need to talk to the associate who shared this book with you to find out how to approach them.

As you share it with enough people who also share it with enough people, your business will grow through word of mouth which is, hands down, the best way to grow *any* business. Ask your doctor, dentist, or any small merchant in town, and they'll agree. You simply can't beat personal referrals.

Would You Share a *Good Deal* With a Friend?

You may now be comfortable with the opportunity, and perhaps would like to share it with your family, friends, and others you know so they can take advantage of it too. How could that benefit you?

First of all, everyone you share this with may not be ready to start their own business. If that's the case, just offer them the convenience of buying at a discount or of being a retail client. This can save them time and the hassles of going out to the stores. You'll make additional income every time they buy something from a catalog or on the Internet! For example, imagine having ten or more retail clients who would buy on a regular monthly basis where you would be paid a bonus, and how that could add to your income!

Again, you haven't retired yet. But you could be making enough for utility payments each month, school clothes, or some special dinners out with the family. First of all, you've bought what you need from your own business, saving yourself time and money. You still have your current job or business. You've also helped a few people you care about save time and money because they're buying from themselves as well. And they can also make money, just like you. Everyone wins!

It's Starting to Get Exciting!
Now say these people begin duplicating what you do. One of your friends, we'll call him Bob, goes out and discovers that four of his friends want to learn more and get started.

Could that make a difference in your life? You're not financially independent yet, but you're on your way! As your business grows, that *extra* each month might be enough to pay your mortgage and maybe even a car payment or two! Imagine that. And basically, all you did was find some people who took advantage of the business, who also found some people who took advantage of it. It's a true win-win situation!

Now you may not yet be making enough extra money to change your lifestyle, but it bears repeating. All you've done is create a monthly personal volume of products based on what you and your retail clients were already purchasing from the stores anyway. You found a few people, who took advantage of the opportunity, while everyone maintained their current job or business.

Now the income from this level of business, by itself, is certainly not wealth. But ask yourself this: "What could I do with a raise that I wouldn't have to put in all the extra hours for?" Could you pay off all your debts sooner? Would you be able to take better vacations? Would the extra bring you closer to retirement with security? *The exciting part is that this income is **in addition to** what you get from your regular job or business!*

Here's Where It *Really* Starts Getting Exciting!

Now, let's get back to Bob. Let's say that as soon as he understands what you understand about this business, he begins duplicating your efforts. Suppose the four friends he shared this idea with decided to go for it and they each share it with only two more who get into the business as well.

Because of the *power of duplication,* your earnings will increase. As a result of Bob's efforts and of all those he brings into your business, who also purchase the products and begin sharing the opportunity, you make money! You would be *leveraging* your time and earning power. It's like being in many places and doing many things at the same time!

Additional income would definitely change things in most homes. How about yours? Remember, you're still working at your current job or business. All you did was change your buying habits and share with others who did the same thing.

The Bigger It Gets, the More Options You Have

You help Bob build his business to a certain level and, as long as you qualify, you'll begin receiving residual income based on all of Bob's present and future volume. As his business continues to grow, so does your residual income check. This is walk-away ongoing income. It can grow long after you've done the work and, perhaps, choose to do no more. Remember the Elvis Pressley and Frank Sinatra estate income situations? You can be earning this money while you play golf, fish, go on vacation, or whatever it is you want to do.

Now when a few of your other associates get to the same level as Bob, it gets even better. As each of your associates builds their business to a certain level, as long as you qualify, it doesn't add to your income, *it multiplies!*

One of the great benefits here is that the people you shared this idea with, who duplicated your effort, aren't the ones who pay you. The corporate supplier pays you directly. Unlike franchising, where you pay more to the master franchiser as you become more successful, the corporate supplier pays you more as you and your other independent business owners become more successful!

As you grow and qualify at different levels, your earnings can equal or exceed that of your current full-time job or other business. If that's not enough, keep going. The more people you share this concept with who, as a result, build a successful business, the higher your residual income becomes. You also participate in more bonus levels.

When you finish this book you will probably want to ask the person who shared it with you to show you exactly how this system works. (Even if you've already seen the concept written out, you may still need to get some questions answered.)

Keep in mind these are only examples. Everyone has different drives, dreams, goals, and commitments and grows at different rates. You may want to do it faster or slower, or just save time and money buying products. Remember, it's your choice and you set the pace.

Should you decide to take advantage of what this opportunity offers you, the following could be your story:

The Short Story of a Former _____ and _____

He was overwhelmed with how many hours he spent at work doing his best to provide for his family. She felt guilty leaving the children in someone else's care while she worked to help make ends meet. When they first saw this opportunity, they secretly hoped it would work, but were skeptical and felt as if they had no time.

As they began meeting other people in this business, they were impressed with the integrity and positive attitudes. Little by little their barriers came down and they made a decision to run for their dreams.

They focused on nothing but succeeding and were willing to do whatever it would take to get them to where they wanted to be. Their attention turned from being only on what was in it for them to making sure that others achieved their goals. Their results have been gratifying.

Today, they live in their dream home and are full-time parents. They travel the world as a family, and are always eager to touch people's lives with this opportunity. Their greatest struggles are behind them now, and the best is yet to come. As someone said, "Their future's so bright, they gotta wear shades!"

Five Things You Could Do *Before* You Get Started

- ◆ Ask the person who shared this book with you if you could see the opportunity again, as it's often a lot to absorb in one sitting. The more you see it the clearer it will become.
- ◆ Next, ask the person who shared this book with you if you could attend a seminar. There you would get more in-depth information and be able to meet some successful associates. What you saw was just a brief overview.
- ◆ Write down all your dreams and goals. Don't let anything hold you back, and assume anything's possible. After you do that, pick your top five, and really imagine how it would be to accomplish them and live your dream.

♦ Next, make a list of people with whom you might like to share this opportunity. They could be anybody from a family member to a dear friend, to a casual acquaintance. Think of all the people you know who you'd like to spend more time with and those you'd like to see grow and prosper. Also consider people who are already quite successful—as they often want to do more.

♦ Finally, thank the person who thought enough of you to share this opportunity with you. Who knows—if they're not already—they could turn out to be one of your best friends.

Are You Living Your Dream?

You've just been introduced to what many consider to be one of the most exciting opportunities in the world for even the average person to get ahead. But it's up to you to do something with it. Nobody's going to twist your arm—the choice is yours. This is simply a vehicle for you to get what you want out of life.

Are you living your dream? Others are living theirs and so can you. *If not this, what? If not now, when?*

And remember...

You're the only one who can sign the death warrant to your dreams!

About the Author

John Fuhrman is a speaker, peak performance trainer, consultant, and international bestselling author. His other books include: *Reject Me—I Love It!, If They Say No Just Say Next!, The Electronic Dream,* and *Dump The Debt and Get Free!* He is founder and president of *Frame of Mind, Inc.,* an organization dedicated to motivation and performance enhancement. John has been an award-winning sales producer featured in *Selling* magazine, as well as a manager and entrepreneur. He is also an award-winning member of the National Speakers Association, and is featured in *Who's Who of Executives and Professionals.*

John's messages are based on his books, personal experiences, and years as a dedicated trainer. He has helped over a million people all over the world improve their performance through his books and speaking programs. John speaks and writes with a special sensitivity to help people grow their businesses and careers and further their personal development.

He is a sought-after speaker and author dealing with such subjects as fear of rejection, failure, success, motivation, e-commerce, as well as sales, leadership, debt reduction, and wealth creation.

For more information on seminars and other training programs or to see if John's programs can fit into your next function, contact Frame of Mind, Inc., 89 Bayberry Lane, Manchester, NH 03104. Telephone John at (888) 883-3303; fax to (603) 622-3859; or e-mail rejectme@aol.com; or you can visit John on the Internet at www.expertspeak.com.

He lives with his wife, Helen, and their two children, John and Katie.

Notes